T.E.Lawrence

Unravelling
The
Enigma

T.E.Lawrence

Unravelling
The
Enigma

By

Dr Andrew Norman

CENTRAL PUBLISHING LIMITED
West Yorkshire

Paperback ISBN 1 903970 19 9

Published
by

Central Publishing Limited
Royd Street Offices
Milnsbridge
Huddersfield
West Yorkshire
HD3 4QY

www.centralpublishing.co.uk

Dedication

To my late friend James Bentley, who said of Lawrence,
"He was my boyhood hero."

Acknowledgements

I am grateful to the following for permission to reproduce or quote:

Pen And Sword Books – Maps 1-4 from 'A Military Atlas Of The First World War' by Arthur Banks (Heinemann Educational Books Ltd. 1997).

The Trustees of The Seven Pillars Of Wisdom Trust for the extracts from the writings of T. E. Lawrence including 'The Mint', 'Seven Pillars Of Wisdom' and the letters of T. E. Lawrence.

'Seven Pillars Of Wisdom' Courtesy of Random House Inc. 1540 Broadway New York.

'Survival' by Christopher B. Smith, courtesy of Perseus Books.

'Lawrence Of Arabia As I Knew Him' by Winston Churchill, Sunday Dispatch, May 19, 1940. Reproduced by courtesy of Curtis Brown Ltd. London, on behalf of the estate of Sir Winston Churchill. Copyright Winston Churchill.

News International Syndication for the quotation from Sunday Times Weekly Review, June and September 1968.

E. M. Forster – talk given on BBC on 1 September 1938 and published in 'The Listener'. Courtesy of Secker and Warburg, Random House Uk Ltd. Norfolk.

Faber And Faber – Siegfried Sassoon's 'Diaries', August 1924.

Gregory Stevens Cox (Editor, Thomas Hardy Year Book) for permission to quote passages from 'The Domestic Life Of Thomas Hardy', Monograph 4.

Heretic Books – 'Male Rape' by Richie McMullen.

Plenum Press – 'Male On Male Rape' by Michael Scarce.

Also to Mrs Jean Norman, Mrs Mary Hurst and Mrs Jane Francis for all their help and encouragement.

PROLOGUE

As I stood looking down at the effigy of Thomas Edward Lawrence in the Church of St Martin's, Wareham, I was struck by the sensitivity captured in the stone face. Something within me connected with this man who had left so many myths behind him when he died dramatically in a motor cycle accident in 1935.

That afternoon, as the sun streamed through the stained glass window and rested on the pale serene face, I decided to make a journey into the past, and try and find out what feeling may have driven this man to take up the sort of life he did.

There are of course many books already written about 'Lawrence of Arabia' - about the battles, the history, his friends and even a book examining him from a psychiatric point of view - but as I explored all this I realised that his psyche was very much misunderstood.

It is easy to see why some people would like to diminish him and his ideology. He did not readily fit into the pattern of an average man, and it is easier to criticise that which we do not understand, rather than admit to the fact that we DO not understand.

For example, Lawrence's alleged dislike of women is very easy to interpret by assuming he was homosexual. In fact by studying his childhood it becomes apparent that he never stood a chance of understanding the opposite sex.

His love for and devotion to the Arab donkey boy Dahoum is easily misread as a tarnished love, when it was really the love of a father-figure for an adopted son.

But always the overriding question in my mind was why, after his heroic exploits in the war, he suddenly chose to shun all thought of further advancement and instead decided to live in anonymity and obscurity in the lower ranks of the armed forces.

As I became more absorbed in his personality, I realised that the only true way to find out about him was not by reading books others had written on him, but by reading first hand what he had written about himself.

If I could only approach his own letters, and his writings - 'Seven Pillars of Wisdom' and 'The Mint' - with an open mind, then somewhere within these works would be locked the 'inner man' - the loyal, honourable, justice-seeking Lawrence with all the hurts and traumas which he tried so desperately to hide and which affected his personal life so deeply.

There was also one other way in which I might be able to reach the 'inner' Lawrence, and that was to investigate his interaction with the many fascinating friends and acquaintances that he had gathered around him through his short but intense life. I would like to invite all who share an interest in Lawrence now to accompany me on this journey to find 'the inner man'.

Chapter 1

HIS MOTHER SARAH

Sarah Lawrence peered through the long sash window of her Victorian house in Polstead Road, Oxford. The mellow red brick building rested quietly, shielded by the leaves and branches of the trees lining both sides of the road.

The afternoons were drawing in with early autumn, and she awaited the return of her four elder sons from school now that another academic year had begun. Her fifth and youngest son, Arnold still remained at home with her.

Her boys were all bright, intelligent and promising. Life in Oxford offered everything she could hope for in the way of education for them, and so in many ways she was happier here than in all her other previous homes, of which there had been many.

Education was of immense value to both Sarah and her husband, Thomas, but it was of particular importance to her, having been brought up in a strict Presbyterian household, where learning, religion and discipline ruled the lives of all within the family.

❧

She sighed contentedly as she awaited the boys' return for tea. Her sons were all doing well at school, but the second eldest, Thomas Edward, otherwise known as 'Ned', was her greatest challenge. Somehow he seemed the one most likely to question her authority, and there were arguments usually resulting in her having to chastise him. What was it about him, she wondered. Why could he not be like the others?

Sarah's life had been hard. Born in Sunderland in 1861, she was illegitimate and when she was only eight or nine her mother died of drink. Thereafter she was brought up in Scotland, first by her grandparents and later by an aunt whose husband was a minister of the church.

In 1879, Sarah joined the household of the aristocratic Chapman family at South Hill, near Castletown Devlin in County Westmeath, Ireland, where Thomas Chapman lived with his wife Edith and their four daughters.

In 1885 Sarah, even though she was fifteen years younger than Thomas, became his mistress and the latter subsequently abandoned his wife and he and Sarah set up home in Dublin thirty miles away. In the same year their son Montague Robert was born.

According to the Matrimonial Causes Act of 1857, legal separation was only permitted if there had been one act of misconduct by the wife or two by the husband. Therefore Mrs Edith Chapman had grounds for divorce but she would not countenance it on account of her strong religious views. In these circumstances Sarah and Thomas adopted the surname of 'Lawrence' and acted as if they were married. However in Ireland the secret of their not being man and wife was impossible to keep. The family moved to Tremadoc in North Wales where, on the 16th of August 1888, their second son Thomas Edward, or 'Ned' as he was known, was born.

Further upheavals were to follow. From Tremadoc they moved to Kircudbright, where in 1889 their third son William George was born, and from there to Dinard on the Normandy coast. In 1893 their fourth son Frank Helier was born in yet another place of residence, the Channel Island of Jersey, and given his second name after its capital town. Finally in 1896 they moved to Number 2, Polstead Road, Oxford, where their fifth and last son Arnold Walter was born in 1900. Here at last the family were able to settle down, even though in the back of Sarah's mind was always the possibility that the secret of their 'living in sin' would be discovered, for in those days such a perceived scandal would lead to a family being ostracised by all sections of the community.

At Polstead Road prayers were said every day, there were frequent readings from the Bible, and three times every Sunday the family attended the church of St. Aldates in the city. Sarah Lawrence objected to drink and made sure that girls were kept at a distance from her five sons.

Driven by a desire to mould the children to her own ways, Sarah disciplined them by a whipping on their bare bottoms. Years later she would tell Lord Astor that his horses would win races only if they were whipped.

She beat Ned frequently, Arnold only once, and the others never. She saw no harm in this, after all was not physical chastisement accepted as commonplace, not only for children in the home and at school, but also for those in the Armed Services and prison inmates? She singled out Ned in particular simply because he was naughtier and more wilful than her other sons. In his grins, smirks and laughter there was a definite rebelliousness which she feared might one day lead him away from that strict religious faith and conformity which she was determined to impose upon him. And what then? Was it conceivable that this seemingly irresponsible youth would one day bring shame on the family? A similar shame to that which she herself had experienced - not only of being illegitimate, but also of knowingly bearing five illegitimate sons? Her own guilt, and a fear of recidivism in her son Ned - was that what led her to whip him so often and so severely?

She wondered whether young Ned 'played up' because he was by nature more sensitive than his brothers, and in consequence felt disorientated and insecure by the family's constant moving of house. Or was it that he felt inferior to them on account of his shortness of stature? At 5ft 6" he was now fully grown. Perhaps he envied them and felt left out. There was Robert, who to her satisfaction had undergone a religious conversion at St Aldate's. He would serve on the Western front, then qualify as a doctor and one day accompany her to China as a medical missionary. Then William, who was tall and handsome and excelled at athletics. He would go up to Oxford to study history, only to be killed in the war. Frank organised the Church Lad's Brigade, of which Ned was also a member. Like Ned he would go on to Jesus College and also be killed in the war. And finally Arnold who, being the youngest, received more attention on that account. Was it attention seeking by Ned that provoked his mother to beat him? No, surely not! Ned was always championing Arnold's cause, and getting into trouble for it. And he would pursue that theme of sticking up for the underdog all his life. But how could she, struggling to bring up five boys, give all of them the emotional love and support they needed? Could it be that Ned enjoyed her beatings? Or if not the beating itself, then perhaps the thought of it. Did he find it in some way exciting? This word 'exciting' was one he himself was later to use to describe his mother.

Sometimes a certain look in Ned's eye made Sarah wonder if he actually despised her - after all had she not taken his father away from his wife? And if he were to guess that he was illegitimate, might he then not despise her even more - even detest her - this hypocritical woman who professes the Christian faith, yet acts in exactly the opposite way? It did not bear thinking about.

And for her part yes, she did not deny certain feelings of jealousy with regard to Ned's warm relationship with his father. As far as their mutual interest in archaeology and history were concerned, she would always be an outsider. Not for her the delights of sharing the long bicycle rides to distant and interesting places which they took together.

And yet her disapproval of Ned was by no means total, for despite his rebelliousness he was not entirely untouched by his Puritanical upbringing. He abhorred those who smoked and drank, had become a vegetarian and viewed physical pleasures as an impediment to intellectual thought. To his credit he lived simply, behaved generously to his friends, and took no interest in the world of materialism.

❦

It was now 1905 and Sarah Lawrence chuckled as she read the latest letter from her son Ned, who was now travelling farther and farther afield. This one described 'a stuffed group including a boa constrictor strangling a tiger' which he had seen in the Norwich Museum. 'Kindly take heaps of love from me to yourself ' he wrote 'and when you've had enough, divide the remainder into three portions, and give them to the three worms (i.e. his brothers) you have with you.' Whether his brothers would chuckle to hear themselves described as 'worms', she rather doubted.

Sarah Lawrence (by unknown photographer c. 1910). Courtesy of J.M. Wilson, provenance: the collection of Theodore Duncan; (identified by A.W. Lawrence as a photographer of his mother).
Courtesy of National Portrait Gallery, London.

T.E. Lawrence and his four brothers during the
Jesus College years. (Left to right: T.E., Frank,
Arnold, Bob and Will.)
Courtesy of Arnold Lawrence.

Two years later he was at Caerphilly in Wales, looking at the 'magnificent' castle. 'The Horn-work is most interesting, and the outworks could not be excelled, either for preservation or attractiveness. There are no good photos to be obtained, and there have been none at any time or at any castle I have visited. The conviction has been continually growing stronger upon me, that I must tour around this part again with a camera.'

His enthusiasm for such ancient artefacts amazed her and she wondered how long it would be before he ventured even further afield, perhaps even abroad. Sure enough, in the same year he wrote from Mont St. Michel in Northern France '.. the stars are out most beautifully, and the moon is, they say, just about to rise. The phosphorescence in the water interests me especially: I have only seen it once or twice before, and never so well as tonight.' And from Chartres Cathedral the following year 'What I found I cannot describe - it is absolutely untouched and unspoilt, in superb preservation, and the noblest building (for Beauvais is only half a one) that I have ever seen, or expect to see.'

∾∾∾

All this talk of the past - of castles and cathedrals - it was his father who would have put these silly notions into his head - told him how his ancestors the Fetherstonhaughs and the Chapmans had once inhabited great castles in Ireland. Perhaps her son Ned dreamed that one day he too would perform heroic deeds like the knights of yore. His admiration for them was obvious, for were not their images, obtained by him from brass rubbings taken from churches all around Oxford, spread across the walls of his bedroom? Why, she thought, could he not live in the present, become a missionary and save souls, as she had always wanted him to do?

❦

It was now 1915. She had written to Ned, who was now working at the Military Intelligence Office in Cairo, shortly after the death of his brother Frank in France, and here was Ned's reply. It did not please her. 'I got your letter this morning' he wrote 'and it grieved me very much. You WILL never understand any of us after we are grown up a little. DON'T you ever feel that we love you without us telling you so? I feel such a contemptible worm for having to write this way about things. If you only knew that if one thinks deeply about anything one would rather die than say anything about it.' She folded it up and replaced it in the envelope. There seemed to be a huge unbridgeable gulf between her and her sons, between her emotional needs and their ability to fulfil them.

Chapter 2

HIS FATHER THOMAS

Thomas Robert Tighe Chapman sank back into his armchair and reflected wistfully on his former life. From where he sat he could see his son Ned out in the back garden polishing the new 3-speed drop-handlebar bicycle which he had recently purchased for him. They had just returned from East Anglia and on the final leg of the journey ridden over 100 miles in a single day.

❧

Born in 1846, Thomas had inherited his late father's estate of South Hill in County Westmeath on the death of his elder brother in 1870. When his cousin died in 1914, he became the seventh baronet and was to be the last.

The Chapmans believed that their estates in Ireland had been granted to them in Elizabethan times through the influence of their distant relative Sir Walter Raleigh, since when the family had retained their English Protestant origins, married into their own circle and mixed little with their Catholic Irish neighbours. Thomas had told Ned of the 'Raleigh' connection, and the boy vowed that he would one day visit Ireland and buy some acres of land in Westmeath, to keep it in the family in honour of the great man. Ned was thrilled to hear tales about his ancestors the Fetherstonhaughs, whose seat was Bracklyn Castle, and the Chapmans of Killua Castle, both in County Westmeath since when his fascination with mediaeval life had known no bounds.

Thomas remembered how his wife Lady Edith, whom he had married in 1873 and by whom he had had four daughters, was nicknamed by the priests variously as 'The Holy Viper' or 'The Vinegar Queen'. This staunch Protestant's crime was to attempt to convert the local Catholics to her own persuasion.

After their separation when Thomas had set up home with Sarah, his life had not been easy. His income had to be divided between the two households which meant having to live on about £400 a year, a sum just sufficient for him not to have to work. However because Edith would not permit a divorce, the couple could never marry.

So there was to be no more shooting, gambling, riding or hard drinking. That was all in the past. His wife Sarah had imposed upon him the strict ways of the Scottish Presbyterian Church and there was no going back. She had remodelled him, forced him to become a teetotaller, and a domestic man who was careful with his pence. His old life and all his friends had gone forever. Now the couple never went calling or socialising, lest anyone discover that they were living in sin.

So here he was, living in comparatively reduced circumstances in middle class North Oxford under the strict Puritanical influence of his common law wife Sarah, having been made to give up his horse for a bicycle. And yet he enjoyed his rides with Ned, and would continue to go with him as long as he was able. Then Ned's schoolfriend 'Scroggs' Benson would have to take over. The lad had also expressed an interest in photography and carpentry, which he Thomas had been able to teach him.

Thomas admitted to himself that one thing he had in common with Sarah was a respect for books, with which the house was full to overflowing, for she, like all good Puritans, knew the value of learning. They had enrolled all of their five boys at Oxford High School, where they were now all doing well.

At school what Ned lacked in height he made up for in fitness and determination, winning prizes for English Language and Literature, History, Divinity and Greek. He also performed well at cricket, gymnastics and cross-country running and in 1907 won the mile race. However there was a down side. He told his father how he had been thrashed for tipping the head-boy's straw hat down over his nose, as he considered the boy a swank. He was asked to apologise but refused. However whilst he was being thrashed, Ned said he kicked the head-boy up the behind so hard that his spectacles came off!

A curious event occurred in the Spring of 1906, which caused his father some anxiety at the time but was soon put right. There was no reason for it, that Thomas was aware of, but Ned suddenly decided to enlist in the Artillery as a private soldier. Was he being bullied at school? And if so, perish the thought, could it be that the secret of his illegitimacy had somehow leaked out? No, bullying was unlikely. After all, few boys were as strong as Ned and none as fit.

However the notion was quickly dispelled and soon he was back in France again and sending his parents accounts of his adventures and telling them of the challenges he was setting himself. 'At Erquy when returning from bathing, I rode a measured half-kilo, on the sand in 40 seconds exactly. There was a gale behind me, and the sands were perfectly level and very fast, but still 30 miles per hour was distinctly good.' However his greatest cycling feat was to come in 1908 when he travelled 2,000 miles through France, and made delightful and detailed drawings of fortresses such as Coucy near Compeigne and Cahors further to the south near Toulouse. And yet he was still not satisfied. '… all the glorious East; Greece, Carthage, Egypt, Tyre, Syria, Italy, Spain, Sicily, Crete... Oh, I must get down here... I would accept a passage for Greece tomorrow' he wrote.

And sure enough in July 1909 Thomas received a letter from Syria. It was Ned's first visit to the Middle East. 'This is a glorious country for wandering in, for hospitality is something more than a name'. And he described the common people as 'each one ready to receive one for a night, and allow me to share in their meals: and without a thought of payment from a traveller on foot'.

In Ireland, Thomas had lived like a lord and enjoyed every minute of it. These sentiments were not however shared by his son Ned. 'Don't go to Ireland, even to play golf' he wrote to his parents in October 1913. 'I think the whole place repulsive historically: they should not like English people, and we certainly cannot like them'.

In 1914 Thomas's financial position eased when his cousin in Ireland died, whereupon the former inherited the baronetcy and a considerable amount of capital. In March 1916 he gave some of this money to his three surviving sons, stipulating that if his son Will, who was officially missing in action, should prove to be alive, then the other three should give back part of their capital so Will might have the same as they had. When it became clear that Will had indeed died, Ned with typical generosity gave £3,000 of the £5,000 his father had given him to Janet Laurie. It was to this lady, a friend of the family, that Ned had once proposed quite out of the blue and without even going through the preliminaries of courting her. The surprised Janet naturally turned down the offer and the matter was never referred to again. She subsequently became attached to Ned's younger brother Will, and the couple had planned to marry. Another £1,000 Ned gave to a friend and the last £1,000 he spent on pictures to illustrate one of his books.

∽∾

Thomas from his armchair could see through the window that Ned had by now finished cleaning the bicycle, but instead of coming inside to rest he was now doing press-ups on the lawn. The lad was forever on the go. He was shortly to go to Jesus College, Oxford where he had been elected to a Meyricke Exhibition to read History, but after that, what occupation or profession could possibly satisfy one with such prodigious energy and diverse interests and talent? His father was not sure what. He only knew that it would be nothing conventional. The answer however was not to be long in coming.

Chapter 3

DOCTOR HOGARTH AND SYRIA

From his study on the first floor of Oxford's Ashmolean Museum, it was a common sight for Dr. David G Hogarth to see a youth, short and of stocky build, running swiftly towards the main entrance. Within seconds that youth would arrive breathless at his door, having taken the stairs two, three or even four at a time. And he would produce from his pocket the inevitable piece of medieval glass or pottery, purchased for a few pence from workmen excavating foundations in the city centre, which he would expect him to identify.

Dr Hogarth enjoyed his position as keeper of Oxford's Ashmolean Museum to which he had been appointed in 1908. Ned - Lawrence that is - was still at school when he first met Dr Hogarth, who had set the youngster to work helping the assistant keeper to identify and catalogue medieval pottery fragments in his spare time.

And now that same youth was maturing into a man. Having already studied the castles of England Wales and France, Lawrence decided that, in order to complete his degree thesis on the influence of The Crusades on the military architecture of Western Europe, it was necessary for him to visit Syria and Palestine and he told Hogarth as much. Hogarth, scholar, archaeologist and author, was twenty-six years older than Lawrence and he himself had travelled widely throughout the Middle East. He had excavated in Cyprus and also in Egypt, under the direction of Professor Flinders Petrie who in 1881 had surveyed the Pyramids and is now generally regarded as the originator of scientific archaeological methods. Dr Hogarth accordingly put him in touch with Charles Doughty the Arabian explorer, who tried to dissuade him as the voyage was 'likely to be most wearisome, hazardous to health and even disappointing.'

Ignoring this advice, Lawrence set out in the summer vacation of 1909 on the S.S.Mongolia, travelling through the Straits of Gibraltar to Port Said and his destination, Beirut.

Here, armed with camera and Mauser pistol and having only a smattering of Arabic he commenced an eleven week trek during which time he walked eleven hundred miles, suffered from flea bites, survived an assassination attempt and contracted malaria. However he was able to visit no less than 36 out of a possible 50 castles, including the famous Kerak des Chevaliers at Hosn, and bring back the photographs, plans and drawings which were to enable him to complete the thesis for the first class honours degree which he was awarded in June 1910.

He subsequently made three visits to France to look at churches and cathedrals and also made a study of the origins of mediaeval pottery for the Ashmolean Museum.

On the recommendation of Dr Hogarth the British Museum applied for and obtained permission from the Ottoman authorities to reopen excavations at Carchemish, an ancient Hittite city built in about 1500 B.C. on the banks of the upper Euphrates just inside the Turkish border. By now Hogarth had taken Lawrence under his wing. From his former college, Magdalen, he obtained for Lawrence a four-year 100 pound-a-year demyship (scholarship) and this would enable his enthusiastic young student to participate in the project.

≪≫

At Christmas 1910 we find Lawrence learning Arabic at the American mission school at Jebail in the Lebanon where in the February Hogarth joined him with what else but supplies of jam, tea and a collection of 'The Classics'! Lawrence learned that the Arabs appreciate and welcome into their group a person who knows even a few words of their language and this was later to stand him in good stead. From here they set off and travelled by way of Haifa, Deraa and Damascus to Carchemish, where Hogarth was to supervise the archaeological dig.

Part of the journey was by train on the Hejaz Railway, which ran from Medina northwards all the way to Damascus, Aleppo and finally Constantinople. Plans to extend this Railway to the holy city of Mecca were abandoned after opposition from patrons of the camel caravans who feared loss of business during the time of the annual pilgrimage to celebrate the birth of the prophet Mohammed. Lawrence could not have known at the time, but soon he was to find himself attacking this railway, rather than travelling on it.

❧❧

In the meantime he was in his element. To his mother in April 1911 he wrote 'Digging is tremendous fun, and most exciting and interesting. The results so far are not nearly enough to justify a second season but the thing is like Pandora's box, with Hope in the last spit of earth. I have had some good pottery lately.' However Hogarth, whom he described 'a most splendid man', was to stay in Carchemish for only two months, March and April, after which he returned to England and supervised the excavation from there.

Hogarth realised that there were those who suspected that his visits to a sensitive area like the Middle East might not be all they seemed - that his interest might not be solely academic. And of course were there ever to be a conflict, he knew that the strategic significance of the area would prove to be of great importance. Some had even suspected him of being a British spy! After all, as a schoolboy he had been at Winchester with Lord Grey the current Foreign Secretary with whom he had kept in close touch. And now, as director of the dig, he and his staff naturally kept their eyes and ears open, but as far as suggestions that he regularly briefed the Foreign Office about the activities of the Turks and Germans in Syria were concerned, well... Hogarth allowed himself the luxury of a smile.

Lawrence spent the 1911 digging season at Carchemish, and it was here that he met 'Dahoum'.

Chapter 4

DAHOUM

There was a boy. Lawrence could not help but notice him. He was looking after the donkeys. He was of slender build and his eyes were large and brown. They followed Lawrence wherever he went. Curious, the latter called him to come over to where he was supervising the exposure of an ancient wall, one which for centuries had been engulfed by the all-pervading sand that was the desert.

The boy was about 14. He spoke to him in Arabic. 'What is your name?' The answer came 'Dahoum' meaning 'the dark one'. 'But that is your nickname. What is your real name?' 'Selim Ahmed' replied the boy shyly, nervous at having been singled out from amongst all the other labourers on the site. But the questions continued. 'Can you read?' The boy nodded and Lawrence jotted down a few words, again in Arabic, which he read hesitantly.

From his appearance, Lawrence guessed he was a mixture of Hittite, the ancient civilisation of northern Syria which included the area where they now were, Carchemish, and Arab. Over the weeks he was able to find out more about him. Dahoum spoke of going to Aleppo to school that was when he had made sufficient money from his work as donkey-boy, ferrying people to and from the site. There was an immediate affinity between the two and Dahoum soon became Lawrence's servant and companion. Lawrence decided to ask Miss Fareedah, a local teacher, to help Dahoum with his reading and writing and loan him a few simple books to begin an education. However Lawrence, perhaps remembering his resentment at his own mother's efforts to mould him to her will, insisted that the boy remain a Moslem. He respected the boy's faith and there was to be no question of him being evangelised.

Lawrence, perhaps looking on Dahoum in the same way as his own father had looked on him, taught the boy photography and made him his laboratory assistant. Then one day they rode out over the plains of northern Syria to visit a Roman palace. The clay of the building had been kneaded with the oils of flowers and the aroma had persisted right up until that time. The guides led Lawrence from room to room saying, 'This is jessamine, this violet, this rose' when suddenly Dahoum said 'Come and smell the sweetest scent of all'. But it was only the desert wind, which they breathed in through open mouths. 'This' he told Lawrence 'is the best: it has no taste.'

It was then that Lawrence began to understand the soul of the Arab. He had lived for a time with the Bedouin, the nomadic tribe who have lived in the Arabian desert for centuries, travelling with their camels, sheep and goats from oasis to oasis. He had adopted their dress of robe, head-cloth, belt and dagger, had gone barefoot, learned to live rough and go for long periods without a wash or a change of clothes. And he had eaten their food of camels' milk and cheese, bread, grapes and figs.

'World-worthlessness' was the common base of all Semitic creeds, and it was this which led them to preach bareness, renunciation, and poverty. There was a homeliness about the Arab God of the Bedouin, who was in their eating, their fighting and their lusting, in fact in all their thoughts. He contrasted this with the Christian God, the God of his upbringing, who was veiled from His followers by their despair of their carnal unworthiness of Him and by the decorum of formal worship.

By all accounts Dahoum was a handsome fellow and a good wrestler. Lawrence had the boy pose for a figure which he himself carved in limestone and displayed in front of his house in the manner of the ancient Greeks.

❧

In the summer of 1913 Lawrence took Dahoum and his site foreman Sheik Hamoudi back to Oxford with him. All three stayed in the bungalow which his father had built for him at the bottom of the garden at Polstead Road, because of the lack of space in the main building. They drew glances as they rode around the city on bicycles wearing their Arab costumes and were astonished when Lawrence took them to London and showed them the underground railway. C.F. Bell of the Ashmolean Museum commissioned the distinguished artist Francis Dodd to paint several portraits of Dahoum, and Lawrence described the first with him sitting down as being 'splendid', the second as 'almost a failure' and the third as 'glorious'.

When in June 1914 Lawrence returned to England, he left Dahoum behind at Carchemish and when war broke out the Turks appointed the latter as guardian of the site, which exempted him from service in the Turkish army. Lawrence was never to see Dahoum again, for a tragedy was to befall the youth which no-one could have foreseen.

David George Hogarth c. 1910.
Courtesy of Mrs Caroline Barton.

Dahoum at Carchemish. C. 1912 photographed by
T.E. Lawrence.
Courtesy of National Portrait Gallery London

Chapter 5

KITCHENER

Herbert Horatio Kitchener looked up from his desk at the fresh-faced, tousled-haired apparition which stood before him, its khaki shirt creased and its tie at half mast. No-one could ever accuse T.E. Lawrence of sartorial elegance! And the great man noticed that this 25 year-old seemed in no way overawed by his presence.

❧

Born in 1850, Kitchener was already on his way to becoming a British institution. A soldier through and through, he had served in the French Army in the Franco-Prussian War whilst still a cadet at the Royal Military Academy. As an engineer officer who knew Hebrew and Arabic, he had worked in Palestine and Cyprus and from 1882 onwards in Egypt where he was to build up forces to avenge the death of General Gordon and defeat the Mahdi in the Battle of Omdurman in 1898. He was appointed Governor General of the Sudan and in 1900 Chief of Staff to Lord Roberts in the Boer War. From 1902 to 1909 he was commander-in-chief in India, and in 1911, by this time field-marshal, he returned to Egypt as British Agent and Consul General. During the Great War he would raise three million volunteers for the army.

He listened patiently as the earnest young man Lawrence expressed his fears about the extent of German penetration into Syria. He was worried, he said, because he foresaw a possible takeover by them of the southern Turkish port of Alexandretta.

And Kitchener had to agree with him. He was well aware that if war came, then a clash with the Turks might well ensue. Therefore the Sinai Peninsula would be a vital buffer-zone against any threatened invasion of Egypt and seizure of the Suez Canal. And events were to prove him right because when in 1915 the Turks did attack, it was the Indian Army's Bikanir Camel Corps who were the first to confront them.

Accordingly Kitchener ordered a topographical survey of the area to be conducted ostensibly under the auspices of the 'Palestine Exploration Fund' but in reality it was to be a spying mission. For this the Turks, who controlled the area around Akaba and Petra, surprisingly enough gave their permission.

Captain Stewart Newcombe of the Royal Engineers led the operation and towards the end of 1913 he was joined in the project by Lawrence and Leonard Woolley, formerly director of the excavations at Carchemish. Lawrence's letter to his mother showed that he was well aware of the real purpose of his mission. 'We are obviously only meant as red herrings' he told her 'to give an archaeological colour to a political job.'

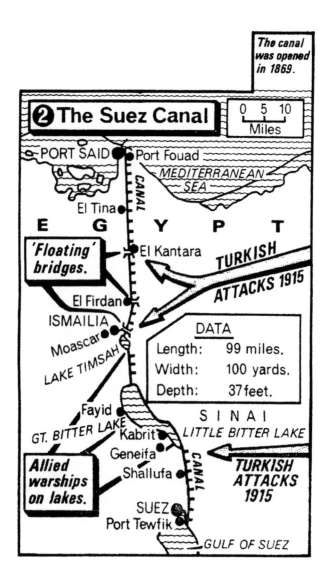

The canal was opened in 1869.

② The Suez Canal

0 5 10
Miles

PORT SAID • • Port Fouad

MEDITERRANEAN SEA

CANAL

El Tina •

E G Y P T

'Floating' bridges.

✕ • El Kantara

TURKISH ATTACKS 1915

El Firdan •

ISMAILIA •

Moascar •

LAKE TIMSAH

DATA

Length: 99 miles.
Width: 100 yards.
Depth: 37 feet.

Fayid •

GT. BITTER LAKE

Kabrit •

Geneifa •

Shallufa •

S I N A I

LITTLE BITTER LAKE

CANAL

TURKISH ATTACKS 1915

Allied warships on lakes.

SUEZ •
Port Tewfik •

GULF OF SUEZ

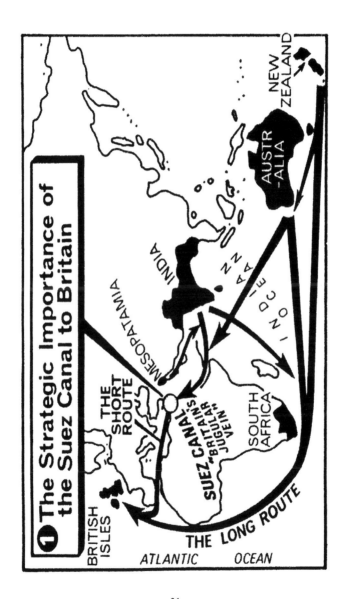

Chapter **6**

EMIR ABDULLAH

Abdullah, with wavy beard and moustache and mournful eyes, peered at the map. He was the second son of Hussein Ibn Ali, Grand Sherif of Mecca, the title 'Sherif' implying that he was a direct descendant of the prophet Mohammed, whose family had ruled for nine hundred years.

In Arabia, different rulers held sway over different regions. Hussein ruled the desert area of Southern Arabia known as the Hejaz, within which territory were the holy cities of Mecca and Medina. It bordered on the Red Sea and its people were the Ateibehs. To the east was Ibn Saud and his Wahabi people and to the north Ibn Rashid and the Shammar.

Persia lay to the east, and Egypt and the Sudan to the west, but it was to Turkey and the Ottoman Empire that the whole of Arabia deferred.

సౌ

Abdullah frowned. The idea had come to him that if the various tribes of Arabia combined, they might rise up and revolt against their Ottoman rulers. He believed that with the help of British and Allied forces, the Hejaz could withstand an attack by the Turks and he therefore decided to approach Lord Kitchener to gauge his reaction. It was February 1914.

At first Kitchener, then Secretary of State for War, was unable to give the assurances that Abdullah required. However they were to be overtaken by events. On August 4th 1914 Britain declared war on Germany and two months later Egypt was declared a British Protectorate. Then, on the 30th of October 1914, Britain declared war on Turkey. Kitchener then informed both Abdullah and his father the Sherif 'Till now we have defended and befriended Islam in the person of the Turks. Henceforward it shall be that of the noble Arab... It would be well if your highness could convey to your followers and devotees who are found throughout the world in every country the good tidings of the freedom of the Arabs and the rising of the sun over Arabia.'

As if this were not enough, he continued 'If Arab nation assist England in this war' he said 'England will guarantee every assistance against foreign aggression.' Abdullah smiled. He was satisfied.

Chapter 7

LAWRENCE'S ROLE

Lawrence had returned to the Carchemish excavations in 1912 and again in 1913. However he was soon to be drawn nearer to the very nerve centre of Arab affairs, where his influence would be not inconsiderable.

When war broke out he found himself attached to the Geographical Section of the General Staff at the War Office. This he owed to the influence of his former mentor Dr Hogarth, who realised his value to intelligence. Here Lawrence spent his time classifying roads and tracks on maps of the area of Sinai. This reinforced his knowledge of an area through which he had already travelled extensively, and the knowledge would later stand him in good stead.

On November 1st the Ottoman Empire declared war on the Allies and soon afterwards Lawrence was commissioned and ordered to proceed to Cairo to join the Intelligence Section attached to General Headquarters, which was under the directorship of Sir Gilbert Clayton.

Lawrence was passionately in favour of Abdullah's idea for an Arab revolt. This would be not only a means of attacking the enemy Turkey, but also, as he told Hogarth, a means to 'biff the French out of all hope of Syria'.

Lawrence meanwhile brought his organisational skills into play. He suggested that a summary of news and information from the various theatres of war in the Middle East be published at regular intervals. The idea was put into effect in the shape of 'The Arab Bulletin', a periodical which was designed to keep the Foreign Office and High Commands in India, Egypt, the Sudan and Mesopotamia fully informed of developments in Arabia. The first copy appeared on the 6th of June, 1916, and Dr Hogarth was its first editor. According to the latter, Lawrence was 'a moving spirit in the negotiations leading to an Arab Revolt and organising the Arab Bureau'.

The Bureau had been established in February 1916 by Sir Mark Sykes who would become co-author of the Sykes Picot treaty. It was housed in the Savoy Hotel and staffed by experts on Arabia and the Arabs. Dr Hogarth, now lieutenant commander, was appointed its director and Kinahan Cornwallis, a former civil servant and now an army intelligence officer, his deputy. The Bureau became the intelligence office for the Arab campaign and Lawrence was to join it from the Cairo Intelligence Section in the November. So once again, Lawrence and Dr Hogarth were united.

Chapter 8

GERTRUDE BELL

Lawrence was sitting under a canopy resting from the heat of the noonday sun with Dr Hogarth's deputy Reginald Campbell-Thompson, and a single lady in early middle age called Gertrude Bell. This was Carchemish in May 1911.

Traveller, author and archaeologist, Miss Bell had managed to irritate Lawrence on this, their first meeting, by telling Thompson that his ideas of digging were 'prehistoric'. She was also full of praise for some German archaeologists whom she had just visited at Qualat Surgar, and in particular for their attempts to 'reconstruct' the buildings they had uncovered.

Lawrence decided to give her chapter and verse on his knowledge of the Hittite civilisation the remains of which they were excavating whereupon she then became, as he states, 'more respectful' and 'on going told Thompson that he had done wonders in his digging in the time, and that she thought we had got everything out of the place that could possibly have been got...' Lawrence described her as 'pleasant: about 36' (in fact she was 43), but 'not beautiful - except with a veil on, perhaps'. Having shown each other all their finds, they parted with 'mutual expressions of esteem' he wrote to his mother.

Born in 1868, Gertrude Bell was the granddaughter of Sir Isaac Bell, ironmaster of a foundry situated on the River Tees in County Durham. She had the distinction of being the first woman to reach the required standard for a first class honours degree at Oxford University, though the degree was not awarded as in those times women were not allowed to be members of the university. She had been drawn to a study of the Middle East by the fact that she had relatives there, and had commenced her travels to the region when she was still in her teens.

In her book 'The Desert and the Sown' published in 1907, she describes her exploration of the Syrian interior. Here she comes across the greatest and most famous of the Crusader Castles, Kerak de Chevaliers, which Lawrence was subsequently to visit in 1910 prior to the submission of his thesis for his university degree. The following year in a letter to her stepmother, she described this 'young man called Lawrence' - he was actually 20 years her junior. 'A pleasant boy' she said 'who is going to make a great traveller'. Because of her extensive knowledge of almost every part of the Middle East, Miss Bell was sent to Basra in Iraq as the Arab Bureau's temporary agent in Iraq whilst Philip Graves attended to Turkish affairs and A.B. fforde represented the interests of India.

❧

A serious setback to the Allied cause occurred in the Spring of 1916 when forces under the command of Major General Charles Townshend, which had previously been successful at Ctesiphon, were cut off at Kut-el-Amara in Mesopotamia having sustained heavy losses. General Gorringe's column which was sent to relieve it was only 20 miles away, but proved incapable of fighting through the Turkish cordon. The men were debilitated by the intense winter cold and lack of supplies, and the Moslem and Hindu soldiers of the Indian detachments preferred to starve rather than eat horse meat. An attempt by Royal Navy River Steamers to break the blockade failed and one of the ships, the 'Junlar' was captured. British aeroplanes made desperate attempts to supply the besieged Division but the quantity of food delivered was insufficient. A last ditch attempt to save General Townshend and his men was devised by General Sir William Robertson, the Chief of the Imperial General Staff.

This was the desperate situation when Lawrence was sent to Basra to meet Reginald Campbell-Thompson, his former colleague from Carchemish, and Gertrude Bell. He arrived there on 5th April and his purpose was to explore the possibility of bribing the Turks and in particular

Jamal Pasha, commander of the Turkish Fourth Army, with a sum not exceeding one million pounds. In return Pasha would be recognised by Britain as ruler of Syria and he would take his troops out of the war.

Referring to this meeting, Miss Bell wrote somewhat tongue in cheek 'This week has been greatly enlivened by the appearance of Mr Lawrence, sent out as liaison officer from Egypt. We have had great talks and made vast schemes for the government of the universe'. One suspects that she was not averse to teasing her younger colleague.

However the attempt failed and on the 29th April 1916, 9,000 troops of the Indian Expeditionary Force which consisted of both British and Indian Army units laid down their arms to Turkish General Khalil Pasha.

Colonel Percy Cox was employed by the Delhi Government as Chief Political Officer of the Anglo-Indian forces in Iraq. He was distrustful of the Arab Bureau and feared that by sponsoring Arab Nationalism it might harm Indian interests in Iraq. However Lawrence persuaded Cox despite the latter's misgivings to take Gertrude Bell onto his staff as the Bureau's corresponding officer.

Gertrude Bell believed in the notion of governing indirectly through local princes, and she saw no reason why this principle should not be applied as successfully in the Middle East as it had been in India. For Lawrence, however, as far as the Arabs were concerned nothing short of complete independence would suffice.

Abdullah with officials at Jidda, October 1916 by
an unknown photographer.
Courtesy of National Portrait Gallery, London.

T.E. Lawrence with Gertrude Bell, Egypt.
Photographed by Maxwell H. Coote.
Courtesy of National Portrait Gallery, London

Chapter 9

SHERIF HUSSEIN

Now elderly, with a long white beard and side whiskers, Sherif Hussein of Mecca was described by Lawrence as 'conceited to a degree, greedy and stupid' but most importantly from the British point of view 'very friendly, and protests devotion to our interests'. 'Reason' wrote Lawrence 'is entirely wasted on him since he believes himself all-wise and all-competent, and is flattered by his entourage in every idiotic thing he does'.

The 'Old Man' as Lawrence called him, had in December 1913 received assurances from the British High Commissioner in Egypt Sir Henry McMahon informing him that he may 'rest assured that Great Britain has no intention of concluding any peace terms of which the freedom of the Arab people from German and Turkish domination does not form an essential condition'.

The Sherif had no reason to love the Turks. Using the Hejaz railway as their lifeline, they had gradually encroached southwards and as they grew stronger were able to garrison the two holy cities of Mecca and Medina with their troops. To add insult to injury they then took the Sherif back to Constantinople to be held there in 'honourable captivity' as Lawrence put it, for nearly eighteen years of his life until he was released by the Young Turks, who had succeeded the Turkish Sultan Abdul Hamid. However this did not prevent Turkey, when she entered the war, from attempting to persuade the Sherif's son Abdullah to join her in a 'jihad' or holy war against the Allies. The Sherif would have none of it and, buoyed up by the news from McMahon that the British would support him, he began to make enquiries.

Upon learning that senior Arab officers serving in the Turkish Army were in favour of the idea of a Revolt, the Sherif sent Feisal, his third son, to Damascus to make contact with the Arab nationalist secret societies. However the latter found the Arabs there were sceptical about the motives of European powers in the area and, as events turned out, rightly so.

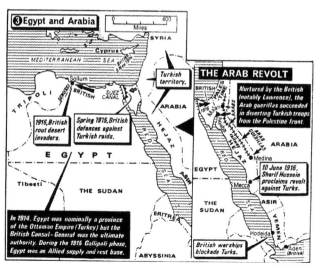

Atrocities by the Turks in Syria and political executions there, together with the reinforcement of their garrison in Medina prompted the Sherif to order Feisal to Mecca so the Revolt could begin, and in early June Ronald Storrs, Dr Hogarth and Captain Kinahan Cornwallis of the Arab Bureau met with Zeid, the Sherif's twenty-year-old youngest son, on an Arabian beach to work out its final details.

∞

The Revolt began on the 10th of June 1916. The elderly Sherif staggered out under the weight of a heavy rifle onto the balcony of his palace in Mecca and fired a token shot at the nearby Turkish barracks. In the following weeks, with the Sherif's sons Ali, Abdullah, Feisal and Zeid acting as field-commanders, Mecca was cleared of Turkish troops. There followed a desperate and unsuccessful rush by the Arabs on Medina, where the Turks terrified and demoralised the former with their artillery and failed to respect the Arab code of warfare by raping and butchering their people, firing houses and throwing living and dead alike back into the flames.

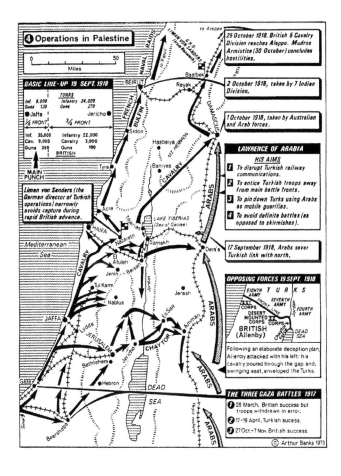

4 Operations in Palestine

0 _____ 50
Miles

BASIC LINE-UP 19 SEPT. 1918

TURKS
Inf. 8,000 | Infantry 24,000
Guns 130 | Guns 270
● Jaffa | ● Jericho
¼ FRONT | ¾ FRONT

Inf. 35,000 | Infantry 22,000
Cav. 9,000 | Cavalry 3,000
Guns 390 | Guns 160
BRITISH

MAIN
PUNCH

Liman von Sanders (the German director of Turkish operations) narrowly avoids capture during rapid British advance.

to Aleppo

LIMAN VON SANDERS (from Nazareth)

NAVAL RAIDS

25 October 1918, British 5 Cavalry Division reaches Aleppo. Mudros Armistice (30 October) concludes hostilities.

Baalbek

Reyak

2 October 1918, taken by 7 Indian Division.

BEIRUT

FRENCH

BULFIN

DAMASCUS

1 October 1918, taken by Australian and Arab forces.

Sidon

Hasbeiya

MT. HERMON

Baniyas

CAVALRY

Tyre

ARABS

LAWRENCE OF ARABIA
HIS AIMS
1 To disrupt Turkish railway communications.
2 To entice Turkish troops away from main battle fronts.
3 To pin down Turks using Arabs as mobile guerillas.
4 To avoid definite battles (as opposed to skirmishes).

Acre

Tiberias

LAKE TIBERIAS
(Sea of Galilee)

HAIFA

CAVALRY

Nazareth

Sarnakh

Dera'a

17 September 1918, Arabs sever Turkish link with north.

Mediterranean Sea

El Afuleh

Beisan

Jenin

Jordan

Jerash

OPPOSING FORCES 19 SEPT. 1918

EIGHTH ARMY / TURKS
FRONT LINE / SEVENTH ARMY
CORPS
DESERT MOUNTED CORPS / CORPS / FOURTH ARMY
BRITISH (Allenby) / DEAD SEA

Following an elaborate deception plan, Allenby attacked with his left: his cavalry poured through the gap and, swinging east, enveloped the Turks.

Tul Karm

Nablus

JAFFA

Es-Salt

Amman

Lidda

JERUSALEM

CHAYTOR

Jericho

Bethlehem

ARABS

DEAD

Gaza

Hebron

SEA

THE THREE GAZA BATTLES 1917
1 26 March, British success but troops withdrawn in error.
2 17-19 April, Turkish success.
3 27 Oct.-7 Nov. British success.

Sinai

Beersheba

ARABS

© Arthur Banks 1973

The Arabs retreated to the hills. Ali went to the Red Sea port of Rabegh to find out why supplies provided by the British were not forthcoming, only to discover that they were being misappropriated by the local chieftain. When Ali's half brother Zeid joined him and the stolen stores were discovered, the two of them were persuaded to opt for a life of plenty and so they left Feisal up country to battle on alone. However a supply of obsolete British guns failed to make a difference and Feisal was forced to withdraw his troops. The start had not been a propitious one.

Chapter **10**

EMIR FEISAL

He (Feisal) was wearing 'long white silk robes' and a 'brown head-cloth bound with a brilliant scarlet and gold cord. I greeted him. He made way for me into the room, and sat down on his carpet near the door. As my eyes grew accustomed to the shade, they saw that the little room held many silent figures, looking at me or at Feisal steadily. He remained staring down at his hands, which were twisting slowly about his dagger'.

This was Lawrence's description of his first meeting with Emir Feisal on the 23rd of October 1916, the name 'Feisal meaning 'the sword flashing downward in the stroke', and 'Emir' meaning chieftain and descendant of Mohammed.

'And how do you like our place here at Wadi Safra?' Feisal enquired. And Lawrence replied tellingly 'Well; but it is far from Damascus'. The implication of Lawrence's words were obvious and everyone sensed it. As he states 'The word had fallen like a sword in their midst. There was a quiver. Then everybody present stiffened where he sat, and held his breath for a silent minute. Some, perhaps, were dreaming of far off success...'

'I felt at first glance' said Lawrence 'that this was the man I had come to Arabia to seek - the leader who would bring the Arab Revolt to glory.' Lawrence, ever a good judge of character, had previously dismissed the Sherif himself as a prospective leader as being 'too aged', and his sons Ali as 'too clean', Abdullah as 'too clever', and Zeid 'too cool'.

The meeting had come about when Lawrence had sought the help of Brigadier General Clayton, Director of the Arab Bureau in Cairo, to allow him to transfer to it from Army Intelligence. One suspects that Lawrence was seeking a more active role in which to direct his boundless energy and talents. In the meantime, when he learned that Ronald Storrs the Oriental Secretary to the British Agency in Egypt planned to visit Jidda west of Mecca on the Red Sea, Lawrence asked if he might go with him. Storr's intention was to meet with Abdullah and discuss the progress of the Revolt, and whilst they were there, Abdullah agreed that Lawrence might meet with his brother Feisal. As Storrs was later to recollect 'I can still see Lawrence on the shore at Rabegh waving grateful hands as we left him there to return ourselves to Egypt. Long before we met again he had already begun to write his page, brilliant as a Persian miniature, in the History of England'. This was a reference to Lawrence's forthcoming book, 'Seven Pillars of Wisdom'.

❧

In the Arab Bulletin of November 1916, Lawrence gives a more detailed description of

Feisal, the man he considered to be 'the leader with the necessary fire, and yet with reason to give effect to our science'. He was 'Tall, graceful, vigorous, almost regal in appearance'. 'Very quick, and restless in movement'. 'Is clear-skinned, as a pure Circassian, with dark hair, vivid black eyes set a little sloping in his face, strong nose, short chin'. Also 'hot-tempered, proud, impatient, sometimes unreasonable, and runs off easily at tangents'. 'Obviously very clever, perhaps not over-scrupulous'. 'Possesses far more personal magnetism and life than his brothers, but less prudence'. And he ends 'A popular idol, and ambitious; full of dreams, and the capacity to realise them, with keen personal insight, and a very efficient man of business'.

Feisal complained that although his force of tribesmen received thirty thousand pounds a month from his father the Sherif, there were 'few rifles, insufficient ammunition, no machine guns, no mountain guns, no technical help, no information'. Lawrence replied that he was there 'Expressly to learn what they lacked and to report it'. Feisal then briefed Lawrence about the history of the Revolt.

From what he had been told and observed, Lawrence concluded that 'the tribesmen were good for defence only' and their keenness on booty 'whetted them to tear up railway lines, plunder caravans and steal camels; but they were too free-minded to endure command, or to fight in a team'. The only way their moral confidence was to be restored after the setback at Medina was 'by having guns, useful or useless, but noisy, on their side'.

Lawrence promised to do his best for Feisal by arranging a base at the Red Sea port of Yenbo where the stores, supplies and armaments he needed would be 'put ashore for his exclusive use'. He then sailed for Egypt where controversy was raging as to whether a brigade of British troops should be sent there also. Lawrence argued vehemently against it, saying that the tribes 'would certainly scatter to their tents again as soon as they heard of the landing of foreigners in force'.

When he returned to Yenbo, Lawrence found Herbert Garland, a Major in the Egyptian Army and a demolition expert who could also speak Arabic, instructing Feisal's tribesmen in 'how to blow up railways with dynamite'.

When Turkish aeroplanes appeared over Rabegh in November, four from the British side were sent to oppose them. Lawrence then set out to impress upon Feisal the need to attack Wejh, a port a further two hundred miles up the coast. Again the pageantry and drama of the occasion did not escape him. Feisal was sitting on his carpet. 'In front of him knelt a secretary taking down an order, and beyond him another reading reports aloud by the light of a silvered lamp which a slave was holding'. Feisal then informed Lawrence that the Turks had managed to 'slip around the head of the Arab barrier forces in Wadi Safra by a side road in the hills, and had cut off their retreat'. The Harb, local tribesmen who formed part of Feisal's army, fled as did the nearby force commanded by the Sherif's youngest son Zeid. The road to Yenbo was 'laid open to the Turks' and Feisal had to rush down to Nakl Mubarak and protect it with five thousand men until 'something properly defensive could be arranged'. Following another Turkish attack, Zeid and Feisal had no choice but to fall back on Yenbo.

When Feisal suggested to Lawrence that he should wear Arab clothes he, finding army uniform 'abominable when camel riding or when sitting about on the ground', readily agreed. He was accordingly fitted out in 'splendid white silk and gold-embroidered wedding garments which had been sent to Feisal lately by his great aunt in Mecca'. Colonel Pierce Joyce, who met Lawrence in Arabia during the war and was later to broadcast for the B.B.C. suggested that it was 'not merely personal vanity' which led Lawrence to adopt Arab costume. 'Arabs have a respect for fine raiment, which they associate with riches and power. It made him an outstanding figure amongst them, excited their curiosity, and therefore increased his authority when dealing with them'.

The growing strength of the relationship between Lawrence and Feisal enhanced the ability of Arabs and British to cooperate with one another. It now remained to be seen whether their combined efforts would be strong enough to defeat their common enemy, the Turks.

Hussein I, King of the Hejaz.

The Emir Feisal, by an unknown photographer,
1919.
Courtesy of National Portrait Gallery, London

Chapter 11

THE ARAB CAMPAIGN

Feisal's stand at Nakl Mubarak had 'only been a pause' and Lawrence was obliged to return to Yenbo 'to think seriously about our amphibious defence of this port'. An attack by the Turks was repulsed with difficulty and meanwhile the tribesmen kept up attacks on the enemy lines of communication until five Royal Naval ships arrived with the purpose of raking any Turkish advance with their guns. The threat succeeded, the blazing searchlights of the ships deterred the Turks from making a night attack, and the crisis passed.

The plan now was to capture the town of Medina and for Feisal to seize the port of Wejh from which further attacks could be made against the Medina-Damascus railway. Feisal's force now ten thousand strong was to be a 'many-tribed' one, the hope being, in Lawrence's words, that 'there would be no more silly defections and jealousies of clans behind us in future, to cripple us with family politics in the middle of our battles'.

Wejh fell to Feisal in January 1917, with the cooperation of Captain Boyle of the Royal Navy who attacked simultaneously by sea with a force of six ships whose fifty guns were directed by a seaplane. The Navy also put ashore an Arab landing party of several hundred men at an undefended place north of the town.

With the fall of Wejh the Turks abandoned their advance on Mecca and fell back to defend Medina and the Railway which was their vital lifeline. The tide was beginning to turn.

Lawrence was not slow to realise the good effect this victory would have on the morale of his forces. Feisal, he wrote, 'was proud, for the advance on Wejh of the Juheina (tribe) was the biggest moral achievement of the new Hejaz government. For the first time the entire manhood of a tribe, complete with its transport and food for a 200 mile march, has left its own diva (homeland), and proceeded into the territory of another tribe with a detached military aim'. From Wejh, Feisal was now able to make contact with the other nomadic tribes in the region and obtain assurances of their loyalty in oaths sworn to him on the Koran.

Lawrence left Feisal's headquarters at Wejh on March 10th 1917 at Clayton's request to visit Abdullah at Wadi Ais. The Turkish commander in the Hejaz had now been ordered to abandon Medina and retire northwards using the railway to transport themselves, their guns and stores. The prospect of these 25,000 Ottoman troops arriving to confront the British line could not be contemplated - by this time the British had crossed the Suez Canal and were making their thrust towards Gaza and Beersheba. Therefore it was decided that Abdullah should attack the Turkish forces. However in the event the Turks at Medina did not move, which gave Lawrence who was incapacitated at Wadi Ais for a month with malaria, the opportunity to rethink the campaign and achieve Clayton's aim of persuading Abdullah to disrupt the Railway.

On the 9th of May Lawrence was sent northwards to Maan, in enemy occupied southern Palestine, to raise the tribes in the area. Clayton reported on this as follows. '... Captain Lawrence has arrived after a journey through enemy country, which is little short of marvellous. I attach a rough sketch illustrating his route. He started from Wejh on 9th May with 36 Arabs and marched via Jauf to Nebk (near Kaf) about 140 miles N.E. of Maan, crossing and dynamiting the Hejaz railway en route. There he met Auda Abu Tayi of the Hueitat Tribe, whom he left at Nebk with instructions to raise men for a raid in the Maan-Akaba neighbourhood'. Lawrence then rode on with only two men through 'very dangerous country to a place near Tadmur where he interviewed Aneizeh Sheikhs.' He went on to destroy a small bridge at Baalbek, visited Druse chiefs at Salkhad and then 'returned to Nebk where Abu Tayi had collected his force of tribesmen'. They then moved to Bair where Lawrence left the Arab force to journey West and then North until he reached the southern shores of Lake Tiberias 'where he inspected the bridges of the Yarmuk Valley'. He returned to Bair having 'destroyed the (Railway) line in various places and derailed a train'.

'From Bair the Arab force (some 2,000 strong) swept the whole country down to Akaba, leaving Maan, but annihilating all the smaller posts including in one place a whole Turkish battalion of some 500 men. The Arabs are now in occupation of Akaba where they have 600 prisoners, including 20 officers and a German N.C.O., and Lawrence estimates the Turkish losses in killed at about 700'.

In the encounter with the Turks at Abu el Lissan, Lawrence inadvertently shot the camel on which he was riding through the head.

Clayton records Lawrence's exhaustion after he had travelled 1,300 miles on a camel in only 30 days, and on the strength of his report, Lawrence was recommended by Sir Reginald Wingate the High Commissioner for Egypt for the Victoria Cross. Instead, however, he received the C.B. (Companionship of the Bath) and was soon afterwards promoted to the rank of Major. It was on the strength of this invaluable Intelligence-gathering by Lawrence that Clayton sent him to meet General Sir Edmund Allenby 'to submit his suggestions to the Commander-in-Chief Egyptian

Expeditionary Force and give the latter all information obtained'.

Chapter **12**

ALLENBY

With the capture of the Red Sea port of Akaba in July 1917, Feisal and his Arab Armies came under the command of General Edmund Allenby, who had commanded the 3rd Army in France from 1915 and had subsequently been given command of the expeditionary force based in Egypt to oppose the Turks. Akaba was thereafter made into an 'unassailable base, from which to hinder the enemy's Hejaz Railway'.

❧❧

Lawrence describes his first meeting with Allenby and one can picture the scene - the Commander in Chief trying hard to know what to make of this young army lieutenant with the permanent grin on his face whose startlingly blue eyes never once met his gaze. '... Allenby was physically large and confident, and morally so great that the comprehension of our littleness came slow to him. He sat in his chair looking at me - not straight, as his custom was, but sideways, puzzled. He was newly from France, where for years he had been a tooth of the great machine grinding the enemy. He was full of Western ideas of gun power and weight - the worst training for our war - but, as a cavalryman, was already half persuaded to throw up the new school, in this different world of Asia...' Lawrence believed that the Arab forces could form the right or eastern flank of Allenby's armies in the advance through Palestine and the latter reacted favourably to this suggestion. 'At the end' says Lawrence 'he put up his chin and said quite directly, 'Well, I will do for you what I can', and that ended it'.

As Lawrence was to write in a letter to his friend Mrs Charlotte Shaw, wife of George Bernard Shaw ten years later, 'All he (Allenby) required of us was a turnover of native opinion from the Turk to the British: and I took advantage of that need of his, to make him the stepfather of the Arab National Movement - a movement which he did not understand and for whose success his instinct had little sympathy. He is a very large, downright and splendid person, and being publicly yoked with a counter-jumping opportunist like me must often gall him deeply'. To Alan Dawnay, another of Allenby's officers, he wrote 'I love him as Petrie (Flinders Petrie the Egyptologist) loves a pyramid - not madly, but in proportion'.

Lawrence then travelled to Jidda to meet Sherif Hussein who agreed that his son Feisal become 'an army commander of the Allied expedition under Allenby'. Allenby for his part summed up the relationship between himself and Lawrence, who now acted as Feisal's liason officer, by saying 'After acquainting him with my strategic plan, I gave him a free hand'.

Whilst Allenby sent 'rifles, guns, high explosive, food and money to Akaba' Lawrence busied himself settling the Howeitat tribe, who he had discovered were in treasonable contact with the Turks, by offering to advance their leader a cash reward - 'something of the great gift Feisal would make him, personally, when he arrived'. He also called for an air attack on the Turkish-held town of Maan, and with the help of British Army sappers, prepared himself for the mining of a train. This was successfully accomplished just outside the town of Hallat Ammar, when the Turks were swept by machine gun fire off the carriage roof tops like 'bales of cotton' and the triumphant Arabs looted, and loaded up their camels with 'mattresses and flowered quilts; blankets in heaps, clothes for men and women in full variety; clocks, cooking pots, food, ornaments and weapons'. Another train was mined near Maan, where Lawrence sustained a flesh wound in his hip from a Turkish colonel firing at him from a window with a Mauser pistol.

Lawrence's 'pupils' became so expert at this type of operation that from one such mined train they captured 'twenty thousand pounds in gold and precious trophies'. As far as the dispositions of the enemy were concerned, Lawrence states with his typical thoroughness and attention to detail '… we knew them exactly; each single unit, and every man they moved'.

∽ formatting ornament ∽

By November 1917 Allenby was poised to open a general offensive against the Turks whilst Lawrence employed the Arabs to attack the Yarmuk Valley Railway and thence hinder their retreat. In Lawrence's words 'Allenby's coming had re-made the English. His breadth of personality swept away the mist of private or departmental jealousies behind which Sir Archibald Murray (Allenby's predecessor) and his men had worked'. Lawrence describes Allenby as 'the man the men worked for, the image we worshipped'.

The River Yarmuk passes through 'a narrow and precipitous gorge' and Lawrence decided that to cut either of the two railway bridges which crossed this river would 'isolate the Turkish army in Palestine, for one fortnight, from its base in Damascus, and destroy its power of escaping from Allenby's advance'. However although two locomotives and three carriages were blown up, Lawrence's party failed to carry the bridge against determined Turkish defenders.

It was shortly after this that Lawrence was captured by the Turks, following Allenby's instructions that he reconnoitre the area around the town of Deraa. Here the abuse and humiliation he suffered at the hands of the Turks would change his life forever.

T.E. Lawrence in Arab robes. Photograph by
Captain R.G. Goslett.
Courtesy of National Portrait Gallery, London

General Allenby IWM
Photograph courtesy of the Imperial War
Museum, London.

Chapter **13**

DISILLUSIONMENT

As he became more and more involved both politically and militarily on the side of the Arabs, so doubts began to form in Lawrence's mind. He had long suspected that British promises to the Arabs had been made more out of expediency than sincerity, and in this he was absolutely right.

Sir Henry McMahon, the British High Commisioner in Egypt, had given a pledge that freedom of the Arab people would be an essential condition of any peace terms concluded with the enemy when hostilities ceased. Yet within a few months secret negotiations were being conducted between Britain, represented by Sir Mark Sykes, France by Georges Picot, and Russia. This was to culminate in the 'Sykes-Picot' agreement, by which Syria, then a larger country than it is today, was to be divided into British and French spheres of influence apart from its coastal region which would come under the control of the French.

Although Lawrence claimed to have had no prior knowledge of the McMahon pledges and the 'Sykes-Picot treaty', which were framed by war-time branches of the Foreign Office he, 'not being a perfect fool... could see that if we won the promises to the Arabs were dead paper. Had I been an honourable advisor' he said 'I would have sent my men home, and not let them risk their lives for such stuff. Yet the Arab inspiration was our main tool in winning the Eastern War. So I assured them that England kept her word in letter and spirit. In this comfort they performed their fine things: but, of course, instead of being proud of what we did together, I was continually and bitterly ashamed'.

Lawrence was to write of his 'agony of mind', 'resentment at my false place', and 'internal perplexities'. 'I've decided to go off alone to Damascus' he said in a note written, but not sent, to Brigadier General Gilbert Clayton 'hoping to get killed on the way: for all sakes try and clear this show up before it goes further. We are calling them (the Arabs) to fight for us on a lie, and I can't stand it'.

Chapter **14**

DEGRADATION

A hand grabbed Lawrence's arm and suddenly he found himself surrounded by Turkish soldiers. Then the gruff voice of their sergeant, speaking in broken Arabic told him 'The Bey wants you' – (Bey being the Turkish word for governor). They ignored Faris, the elderly peasant who had accompanied Lawrence on his mission to reconnoitre the town of Deraa, presently under Turkish occupation. The two had already found German stores and rudiments of trenches, and Turkish troops and their tents. Also an aerodrome and sheds containing Albatross aircraft.

Lawrence replied also in Arabic to the officer who had now arrived on the scene, and pretended to him that he was a Circassian (one from an area in the northern Caucasus). The Turks responded to this by accusing him of being a deserter. Lawrence countered by pointing out that Circassians are not required to perform military service. Finally the officer said he did not believe him and told him he was to be enrolled for that very thing.

That evening after being fed and washed, Lawrence was taken to the bedroom of the Bey, a 'bulky man' who ' sat on the bed in a night-gown, trembling and sweating as though with fever'.

Suddenly the Bey pulled Lawrence down onto the bed and a wrestling match took place in which Lawrence, despite his small stature, gave a good account of himself. When the Bey offered to make him his orderly and even pay him wages if he, Lawrence 'would love him', the latter refused and pushed him away. The Bey cursed 'with horrible threats' and began to paw Lawrence, whereupon the latter jerked his knee into him. Three soldiers appeared and whilst they held Lawrence down, the Bey hit him repeatedly in the face with his slipper and then penetrated his flesh with a bayonet.

'You must understand that I know: and it will be easier if you do as I wish' said the Bey. At first Lawrence was dumfounded, and thought at first that the Bey had guessed his identity, but on reflection he decided to put it down to 'a chance shot' on the part of his adversary. He was then stretched over a bench whilst the corporal flogged him with 'a whip of the Circassian sort, a thong of supple black hide, rounded and tapering from the thickness of a thumb at the grip down to a hard point finer than a pencil'. At first Lawrence refused to cry out, but when eventually he was forced to, he used only Arabic so as not to give himself away. Finally he states 'a merciful sickness choked my utterance'. Then, as he was being kicked, he felt 'a delicious warmth, probably sexual, was swelling through me ...'

After more kicking and beating 'the next I knew I was being dragged about by two men, each disputing over a leg as though to split me apart:

while a third man rode me astride. It was momentarily better than flogging'. Then Nahi (that was the Bey's name) called and Lawrence was cleaned up and taken to his bed, but he now rejected the latter as being 'too torn and bloody'. Lawrence was then taken to another room where his wounds were washed and bandaged.

The following morning to his surprise he had no pain. Donning the 'suit of shoddy clothes' which hung on a door, he climbed out of the window and 'went shaking down the road towards the village'. He made his escape through a hidden valley which he made a mental note of because he believed (correctly) that it might later be used to advantage by his forces 'to attain Deraa town secretly, and surprise the Turks'.

'... in Deraa that night' wrote Lawrence 'the citadel of my integrity had been irrevocably lost'.

Chapter 15

ON TO VICTORY

When Lawrence flew northwards to Suez and arrived at Allenby's headquarters beyond Gaza intending to tell him of the failed attack on the Yarmuk bridge, 'word came from Chetwode (General Sir Philip Chetwode, one of Allenby's commanders) that Jerusalem had fallen, so 'the miserable details of failure could remain concealed'. Allenby, says Lawrence, 'was good enough, although I had done nothing for the success, to let Clayton (Brigadier General Gilbert Clayton) take me along as his staff officer for the day'. The 'ceremony at the Jaffa Gate' was, for Lawrence, 'the supreme moment of the war'.

✧✦✧

Jerusalem had fallen to the Allies on December 9th 1917. Allenby and Lawrence then agreed a plan whereby the following February the former would advance towards Jericho whilst the latter organised a thrust by the Arabs towards the Dead Sea. All being well the two forces would then meet and join forces in the Jordan Valley at the end of March.

However on the 21st of March there began a German onslaught on the Western Front, as a result of which troops were removed from Allenby's theatre of operations to be sent to Flanders to stem the enemy's advance there. He was now ordered to go on the defensive, and the attack would have to be postponed whilst his army was rebuilt with Indian troops and Indian divisions from Mesopotamia. For the moment, he told Lawrence, we must both just hold on. When the Imperial Camel Brigade in Sinai was disbanded Lawrence, now Lieutenant Colonel, asked Allenby if he might have their 2,000 camels 'To put a thousand men into Deraa any day you please', as he told his chief. Allenby smiled and the wish was granted.

In Lawrence's words, Allenby's army 'marched and fought nearly to a standstill, in the ledged and precipitous hills, shell-shocked and bullet-spattered, amid which they wrestled with the Turks along a line from Ramleh to Jerusalem' with Feisal's Arab armies supporting its right flank.

The arrival of armoured cars, driven by British crews, gave the Allies a hitherto undreamt of mobility. They were used not for close encounters, instead they stood off and softened up their targets by firing from a distance before the camel corps moved in to finish the work.

Lawrence paid his men six pounds a day, but provided them with his own camels so their money was 'clear income'. However such was the enmity between the men of the thirty tribes that 'nearly sixty of them died', or in other words murdered one another, whilst in Lawrence's service.

Whilst Allenby's forces were taking Jericho, Lawrence's were halted when money to pay Feisal's army of forty thousand men was diverted by Sherif Hussein's son Zeid, who had been influenced by dishonest advisors.

A dejected Lawrence left Tafileh and rode the eight miles to Beersheba to acquaint Dr Hogarth of the bad tidings. He took full responsibility, told Hogarth he had 'made a mess of things' and proposed to ask General Allenby to find him 'some small part elsewhere'. 'My will had gone' wrote Lawrence 'and I feared to be alone, lest the winds of circumstance, or power, or lust, blow my empty soul away'. Dr Hogarth was himself aware of Arab deficiencies, describing 'the nomad's acute distaste for sustained action and winter campaigning'. 'Nowhere as yet', he stated 'have the Arabs held on for more than three days at the outside, to any (railway) station or other point captured on the line, nor have they wrecked any of the larger bridges'. Zeid, he said, was deterred by the 'continued cold... nervousness about operating in a new country... but most of all by the natural inertia and weakness of purpose which he shares with some of his brothers'.

Clayton, however, convinced Lawrence of Allenby's continuing need for the Arab forces and therefore, in Lawrence's words 'There was no escape for me. I must take up again my mantle of fraud in the East'.

Meanwhile, hit and run attacks against Turkish blockhouses, outposts and telegraph and telephone lines continued, with the ever-present danger of running into enemy patrols. Trained 'dynamiters' blew up the bridges and derailed the trains of the Hejaz railway which deprived the Turks of vital food, arms and ammunition, and Arab forces claimed a great success when they severed the line permanently between Maan and Medina. This had the effect of isolating the twelve thousand strong Turkish garrison of Medina and preventing it from moving against General Allenby.

જીજ્જી

For the last year and a half Lawrence had spent his time 'riding a thousand miles each month upon camels, with added nervous hours in crazy aeroplanes, or rushing across country in powerful cars'. In his last five actions 'I had been hit, and my body so dreaded further pain that I had to force myself under fire'. The cold, hunger, frost and dirt had 'poisoned my hurts into a festering mass of sores'.

He continued to agonise over his part in the Revolt. 'Today it came to me with finality that my patience as regards the false position I had been led into was finished. A week, two weeks, three weeks, and I would insist upon relief. My nerve had broken; and I would be lucky if the ruin of it could be hidden so long'. As the palm trees quivered in the gentle breeze the ground, like sand beneath his feet, was about to shift.

However, despite his suspicions of an impending betrayal of the Arabs by the Allies, Lawrence clung to the hope that he could help them. 'I salved myself with the hope that, by leading these Arabs madly in the final victory I would establish them, with arms in their hands, in a position so assured (if not dominant) that expediency would counsel to the Great Powers a fair settlement of their claims'.

And when the Arabs cut the railway out of Deraa, he decided 'They (the Arabs) had joined the war to win freedom, and the recovery of their own capital by force of their own arms was the sign they would best understand ... Therefore, for every sensible reason, strategical, tactical, political, even moral, we were going on'.

And so despite his near exhaustion, he was dispatched to Akaba from Cairo to 'make my new terms with Feisal' and plan for the forthcoming attack on Maan. However progress was impeded because of the strength of its Turkish garrison.

∽∾

In July Allenby, whose confidence Lawrence describes as being 'like a wall', was planning with the latter an autumn offensive in which he would trick the Turks into thinking he was building up his forces in the Jordan Valley, whilst the real attack would come in Palestine, whose railway communications were to be cut by the Arabs.

Lawrence's praise for Feisal during these arduous and uncertain days was unbounded. During the two years he 'laboured daily', urging his men to 'compose their feuds' until 'there was no blood feud left active in any of the districts through which he had passed, and he was Court of Appeal, ultimate and unchallenged, for Western Arabia'.

Feisal mediated and gave judgments in disputes, put down a mutiny by running barefoot into the midst of the mutineers and 'laying about them with the flat of his sword like four men', and 'laboured night and day at his politics'. As more and more volunteers and great sheiks rode in to swear allegiance, he made them swear solemnly on the Koran 'to wait while he waited, march when he marched, to yield obedience to no Turk, to deal kindly with all who spoke Arabic and to put independence above life, family and goods'.

'No Arab ever impugned his judgements, or questioned his wisdom and competence in tribal business. By patiently sifting out right from wrong, by his tact, his wonderful memory, he gained authority over the nomads from Medina to Damascus and beyond'.

Lawrence made a comparison between the two leaders, Arab and British. Whereas Feisal 'was a brave, weak, ignorant spirit, trying to do work for which only a genius, a prophet or a great criminal, was fitted', Allenby, says Lawrence enigmatically, 'came nearest to my longings for a master, but I had to avoid him, not daring to bow down for fear lest he show feet of clay with that friendly word which must shatter my allegiance'.

It was on September the 18th 1918 that Lawrence and the Arab armies, backed up by aeroplanes and armoured cars supplied by the British, cut the three railway lines out of Deraa where Lawrence had undergone his humiliation at the hands of the Turkish Bey. At the same time he feigned an attack in this area, whilst the following day Allenby, whose army included 9,000 French troops and the Australian 3rd Light Horse, made his main thrust along the coast. The Turkish armies were 'scattered beyond recovery' and on the 1st of October, Allenby entered Damascus unopposed and parked his grey Rolls-Royce outside the Victoria Hotel The city, says Lawrence, was 'mad with joy'.

The fall of Damascus was to the Arabs and event of immense significance. Not only did they regard the city as the 'capital' of the desert but, as Gertrude Bell the English traveller and author had written in 1907, the city 'holds and remembers the greatest Arab traditions'.

However Dr Hogarth, perhaps foreseeing the inevitable religious squabbles which would ensue over the capture of the city, was more sanguine in his appraisal and described it as 'a great, but a very thorny acquisition'.

Chapter **16**

DISCORD

Lawrence describes the first meeting between Emir Feisal and General Allenby, when the former arrived from Deraa. 'It was fitting the two chiefs should meet for the first time in the heart of their victory; with myself acting as the interpreter between them'. Feisal thanked the Commander-in-Chief 'for the trust which had made him and his movement. They were a strange contrast: Feisal, large-eyed, colourless and worn, like a fine dagger; Allenby, gigantic and red and merry, fit representative of the Power which had thrown a girdle of humour and strong dealing round the world'.

However the Australian Major General Sir Harry Chauvel described what happened when Allenby, with Lawrence acting as interpreter, acquainted Feisal with the terms of the Sykes-Picot Agreement. Feisal would govern Syria, under France as the protecting power, and make the day to day decisions in co-operation with a French liaison officer who would work with Lawrence. Lebanon and Palestine however would be controlled directly by Britain and France. Feisal objected strongly, saying he had been advised by Lawrence that the Arabs were to have the whole of Syria including Lebanon but excluding Palestine. Chauvel records 'The Chief (Allenby) turned to Lawrence and said: 'But did you not tell him that the French were to have the Protectorate over Syria?' Lawrence said: 'No sir, I know nothing about it.' The Chief then said: 'But you knew definitely that he, Feisal, was to have nothing to do with the Lebanon?' Lawrence said: 'No, sir, I did not.' 'After Feisal had gone, Lawrence told Allenby that he would not work with a French liaison officer and that he was due for leave and thought he had better take it now and go off to England. The Chief said, 'Yes! I think you had!', and Lawrence left the room.'

However Allenby did furnish Lawrence with a letter of introduction to the King's equerry and also one for the Foreign Office, to enable him to explain the Arab position once he had returned to England.

And so three days after the fall of Damascus Lawrence returned to Cairo and thence to England. In the meantime the Allied forces captured Beirut, Homs, Hama and Aleppo and by the time the Turkish armistice was signed on October 31st, occupied almost all of Syria and Mesopotamia.

Colonel Pierce Joyce, one of the English officers who commanded the Egyptian troops which were with Sherif Hussein and who helped train regular forces being assembled at Rabegh, gave his opinion as to why Lawrence was such a successful leader. 'It was not, as is often supposed, by his individual leadership of hordes of bedouin that he achieved success in daring ventures, but by the wise selection of tribal leaders and providing the essential grist to the mill in the shape of golden rewards for work well done'.

As for General Allenby, he was appointed British high commissioner for Egypt in 1919, in which capacity he served until 1925.

∿

Lawrence regarded Allenby as the professional soldier par excellence and although Allenby did not hesitate to grant Lawrence his wish to return to England once the latter had made it clear that he was not in sympathy with Britain's post-war strategy vis-à-vis the French, the Commander-in-Chief did have the wisdom to recognise the strength and sincerity of Lawrence's feelings and provide him with the means to express them to those that mattered once he had returned home.

Chapter 17

CHURCHILL AND THE PARIS PEACE CONFERENCE

Winston Churchill was born in 1874 and educated at Harrow School and Sandhurst. Having served with the Spanish forces in Cuba he joined the British Army in India and in 1898 was sent to the Sudan and took part in the Battle of Omdurman. During the Boer War when he was correspondent of the 'Morning Post' he was captured but escaped, and returned to England a hero. In 1900 he was elected to the House of Commons.

From 1906 he served in Campbell-Bannerman's Liberal Government in various capacities as Under Secretary for the Colonies, President of the Board of Trade, Home Secretary and First Lord of the Admiralty. After the disastrous Allied landings at Gallipoli in 1915 which he planned, he resigned and in 1916 served in France with the Royal Scots Fusiliers.

In 1917 he was recalled to office by Prime Minister Lloyd George and became Secretary of State for War and for Air from 1919 to 1921 and Colonial Secretary from 1921 to 1922.

Churchill first met Lawrence early in 1919, prior to the Paris Peace Conference, and took the opportunity to deliver a rebuke to him in the mistaken belief that he had snubbed the monarch King George V at a public ceremonial. The occasion referred to was Lawrence's refusal to accept from the King, whom he had met on Allenby's introduction the previous October, the decorations of C.B. (Companion of the Most Honourable Order of the Bath) and D.S.O. (Distinguished Service Order). Only later did Churchill learn that in fact Lawrence and the King had at the time been alone together, and that the former had begged that he might be allowed to refuse the medal and insignia. This behaviour by Lawrence was not without precedent - other medals and honours awarded but returned by him were the 1914-18 Star, War Medal, Victory Medal with Oak Leaves, Légion d'Honneur, Croix de Guerre with Palms and Italy Service Medal.

This action by Lawrence made a great impression on Churchill, who wrote in the 'Sunday Dispatch' in an article entitled 'Lawrence of Arabia as I knew him', the following words. 'This was the only way in his (Lawrence's) power... of rousing the highest authorities in the State to a realisation of the fact that the honour of Great Britain was at stake in the faithful treatment of the Arabs. The King himself should be made aware of what was being done in his name, and he knew no other way'. Churchill also gave Lawrence credit for his action, which had opened his

(Churchill's) eyes 'to the passions which were seething in Arab bosoms'.

Churchill went on to describe his subsequent meeting with Lawrence at the Paris Peace Conference, which opened at Versailles on the 18th of January 1919. This the latter attended in the role of technical advisor to the British delegation and interpreter and link-man between the Allied Powers and Emir Feisal, who arrived with his entourage from the newly-independent territory of Hejaz. 'He (Lawrence) wore his Arab robes, and the full magnificence of his countenance revealed itself. The gravity of his demeanour, the precision of his opinions, the range and quality of his conversation all seemed enhanced to a remarkable degree by the splendid Arab head-dress and garb. From amid the flowing draperies his noble features, his perfectly chiselled lips and flashing eyes loaded with fire and comprehension shone forth. He looked what he was - one of nature's greatest princes. We got on much better this time, and I began to form that impression of his strength and quality which since has never left me. Whether he wore the prosaic clothes of English daily life, or afterwards in the uniform of an Air Force mechanic, I always saw him henceforward as he appears in Augustus John's brilliant pencil sketch'.

Lawrence's views on what should happen in the Middle East after the war was over were well known. The previous autumn he had proposed to the Eastern Committee of the British War Cabinet that the sons of the Sherif of Mecca should be made the post-war rulers of Syria and

Mesopotamia, rather than the French or the Indian Governments who wished these territories to come under their respective spheres of influence. Such was his strength of feeling on the subject that he wrote articles in the 'Times' newspaper publicising the role Feisal and the Arabs had played in the war. He also spent much time promoting his ideas to President Woodrow Wilson and the American delegation whom he met in the hope that the Americans, whom he regarded as a more benign influence than the French, might take responsibility for Syria. However, in Churchill's words 'The idea that France, bled white in the trenches of Flanders, should emerge from the Great War without her share of conquered territories was insupportable to Clemenceau (the French prime minister) and would never have been tolerated by his countrymen'. Also Britain felt it necessary to make concessions to France, in order to protect her access to the Mesopotamian oil fields. And so after three months of wrangling between Lloyd George and Clemenceau, it was finally agreed that the mandate for a reduced Syria and Lebanon should be awarded to France, and when the Arabs resisted the French reacted by expelling Feisal from Damascus.

Great Britain was assigned the mandate for Iraq, which led the following month to a tribal rebellion and much loss of life. Of this Lawrence, the arch proponent of Arab self-government, wrote 'How long will we permit millions of pounds, thousands of Imperial troops, and tens of thousands of Arabs to be sacrificed on behalf of a form of colonial administration which can benefit nobody but its administrators?'

Lawrence also participated in the Allied negotiations with Zionist leader Chaim Weizmann regarding the proposed creation of a Jewish national home in Palestine and the immigration there of eighty thousand Jews annually. When Felix Frankfurter, professor of law at Harvard who represented the Zionists and Feisal met, it was Lawrence who was asked to draft the letter summarising Feisal's views. This letter, published in the New York Times on March 5th, contained sentiments like 'working together for a reformed and revived Near East', 'there is room in Syria for both of us' and wished 'the Jews a most hearty welcome home'. The contents of this letter which, according to Frankfurter, 'has ever since been treated as one of the basic documents affecting Palestinian affairs and Arab-Jewish relations', has been argued over ever since. Feisal, who had represented his father Sherif Hussein at the Peace Conference, did not disavow its authorship, but his enthusiasm for it may have been lessened when the British failed to support him over Syria. Britain was assigned the mandate for Syria, which she kept until 1948 when she had to abandon it and the State of Israel came into being.

On April 7th 1919 a telegram arrived for Lawrence telling him that his father Thomas was ill. He returned at once to England but only to find that his father had already died.

And so when the Treaty of Versailles was signed on the 28th of June 1919, Lawrence's worst fears were realised. There was a failure to grant political freedom to the Arabs, previously under the rule of the Ottoman Empire, who were instead now placed under the British and French in mandated territories under the League of Nations.

The Bay Of Deraa (centre), with his officers. January 1918.
Targan Carikli.

Delegates from the Cairo Conference on a visit to the Pyramids, 20th March 1921. Those present included (from left to right): Clementine Churchill, Winston Churchill, Gertrude Bell, Lawrence and Churchill's detective. Photographed by G.M. Georgoulas.
Courtesy of National Portrait Gallery, London

Chapter **18**

'SEVEN PILLARS OF WISDOM'

In November 1919 Lawrence who, through over-generosity to his friends, was in a desperately impecunious state was elected, through the influence of Geoffrey Dawson who was to become editor of the 'Times' newspaper, to a seven-year fellowship of All Souls College, Oxford. Ostensibly this was with the object of researching into the 'antiquities and ethnology and the history of the Near East', but in reality it was to enable him to complete his book 'Seven Pillars of Wisdom' about the war, of which by the May of 1922 he had completed the third draft and had had eight volumes printed in Oxford.

The beauty and elegance of Lawrence's style of writing complements in 'Seven Pillars' his meticulous attention to detail, born of a keenness of observation in regard to enemy encampments, troop dispositions, nature of terrain and so forth. For example, of the mountains of Rumm he writes 'The crags were capped in nests of domes, less hotly red than the body of the hills; rather grey and shallow. They gave the finishing semblance of Byzantine architecture to this irresistible place: this processional way greater than imagination. The Arab armies would have been lost in the length and breadth of it, and within the walls a squadron of aeroplanes could have wheeled in formation. Our little caravan grew self-conscious and fell dead quiet, afraid and ashamed to flaunt its smallness in the presence of the stupendous hills'.

Churchill was to write of 'Seven Pillars' in glowing terms. 'As a narrative of war and adventure, as a portrayal of all that the Arabs mean to the world, it is unsurpassed. It ranks with the greatest books ever written in the English language. If Lawrence had never done anything except write this book as a mere work of the imagination his fame would last - to quote Macaulay's hackneyed phrase - as long as the English language is spoken in any corner of the globe. When most of the vast literature of the Great War had been sifted and superseded by the epitomes, commentaries and histories of future generations...Lawrence's tale of the revolt in the desert will gleam with immortal fire.'

Lawrence presented Churchill with two copies of the book, which he refused payment for. The first bore the inscription -

'Winston Churchill, who made a happy ending to this show.
T.E.S.'

and the second -

'W.S.C. And eleven years after we set our hands to making an honest settlement, all our work still stands, and the countries having gone

forward, our interests having been served, and nobody killed, either on our own side or the other. To have planned for eleven years is statesmanship. I ought to have given you two copies of this book!

T.E.S.'

It was at All Souls that Lawrence began collecting poems including five by Thomas Hardy, three by Siegfried Sassoon and others by Walter de la Mare and Robert Graves whom he met at a college guest night in that same month. Graves was later to introduce him to Edmund Blunden, John Masefield the poet laureate, Robert Bridges and the artist and sculptor Eric Kennington.

Chapter **19**

CHURCHILL MAKES AMENDS

When in the spring of 1921 Churchill was appointed Colonial Minister with responsibility for overseeing British interests in the Middle East, he offered Lawrence the position of his advisor which the latter accepted. According to Churchill, this 'presented a most melancholy picture. Half a dozen very able men from the India Office and those who had served in Iraq and Palestine during the war formed the nucleus. I resolved to add Lawrence to their number, if he could be persuaded'. The outcome was successful, and Churchill goes on to say 'Accompanied by Lawrence, Hubert Young a regular soldier fluent in Arabic whom Lawrence had first met at Carchemish and Trenchard from the Air Ministry, I set out for Cairo. We stayed there and in Palestine for about a month. We submitted the following main proposals to the Cabinet. First we would repair the injury done to the Arabs and to the House of the Sherifs of Mecca by placing the Emir Feisal on the throne of Iraq as King, and by entrusting the Emir Abdulla (Feisal's brother) with the government of Trans-Jordania (now Jordan). Secondly we would remove practically all the troops from Iraq, and entrust its defence to the Royal Air Force. Thirdly we suggested an adjustment of the immediate difficulties between the Jews and Arabs in Palestine'.

∽👁👁∾

The way Lawrence was able to 'sink his personality, to bend his imperious will, and pool his knowledge in the common stock' was, Churchill states, 'One of the proofs of the greatness of his character and the versatility of his genius. He saw the hope of redeeming, in a large measure, the promises he had made to the Arab chiefs, and of re-establishing a tolerable measure of peace in those wide regions'. And he continues, 'One day I said to Lawrence 'What would you like to do when all this is smoothed out? The greatest employments are open to you if you care to pursue your new career in the Colonial Service.' He smiled his bland, beaming, cryptic smile and said 'In a few months my work here will be finished.' 'But what about you?' said Churchill, and the reply from Lawrence was 'All you will see of me is a cloud of dust on the horizon.'

So now, from being a victorious war hero who moved in high circles, T.E. Lawrence was to embark on a course of anonymity and self-effacement

There was a moment of light relief however when, at the end of the Peace Conference in Cairo in March 1921, Lawrence, Trenchard, Churchill and Gertrude Bell rode on camels to the Pyramids to have their photographs taken. Churchill duly fell off his camel and insisted on remounting, whereupon Lawrence shook with laughter.

Chapter **20**

DREAM AND REALITY

Lawrence summarised his motives in choosing to play his key role in the Arab Revolt in a letter he sent confidentially to the Foreign Office official G.J. Kidston on the 15th of November 1919 but which was only made public in 1968. They were fourfold - 'Personal, in that I liked a particular Arab very much (this presumably was Dahoum), and I thought freedom for the race would be an acceptable present - Patriotic. I wanted to help win the war, and Arab help reduced Allenby's losses by thousands - Intellectual curiosity. I wanted to feel what it was like to be the mainspring of a national movement, and so to have half a million people expressing themselves through me: and being a half poet, I don't value material things much. Sensation and mind seem to me much greater, and the ideal, such a thing as the impulse that took us into Damascus, the only thing worth doing' - and finally 'Ambition. You know how Lionel Curtis (Fellow of All Souls College, Lecturer in Colonial History who had corresponded constantly with Lawrence since 1923) has made his conception of the Empire - a commonwealth of free peoples - generally accepted. I wanted to widen that idea beyond the Anglo-Saxon shape, and form a new nation of thinking people all acclaiming freedom, and demanding admittance into our Empire. There is to my mind no other road for Egypt and India in the end, and I would have made their path easier by creating an Arab Dominion in the Empire. I don't think there are any other reasons.'

However he goes on to state that the first motive - 'personal' - 'had died some weeks before, so my gift was wasted and my future doings indifferent on that count', the second - 'patriotic' - 'was achieved, for Turkey was broken and the Central Powers were so unified that to break one was to break all', the third - 'intellectual curiosity' - 'was romantic mainly and one never repeats a sensation. When I rode into Damascus the whole countryside was on fire with enthusiasm, and in the town a hundred thousand people shouted my name. Success always kills hope by surfeit' and the fourth - 'ambition' - 'remained, but it was not strong enough to make me stay. If you want to make me work again you would have to recreate motives i) and ii). As you are not God, motive i) is beyond your power'.

And he ends - 'I never told anyone before, and may not again, because it isn't nice to open oneself out. I laugh at myself because giving up has made me look so futile'.

In July, August and September 1921 Lawrence was in Jidda trying, without success, to persuade Sherif Hussein of the Hedjaz to accept the terms of the Cairo Peace Settlement. Lawrence himself did not find this task an easy one and described the visit as 'the beastliest trip ever I had'.

In 1924 Sherif Hussein was ousted by his rival Arabian leader Ibn Saud of Riyadh, who had always resisted the Sherif's claim to be King of the Arabs and whose Wahhabi tribesmen had invaded the Hejaz and defeated the Sherif's forces in May 1919. Ibn Saud's forces now overran Mecca, obliging the Sherif to go into exile first to Akaba and then to Cyprus. In 1930 when the Sherif had a stroke, the British Government allowed him to go to Amman to end his days near his sons.

Emir Ali, eldest son of Sherif Hussein who succeeded his father as King of the Hejaz, reigned for only a few months before fleeing to Baghdad where he spent the remainder of his days as a pensioner of his brother Feisal. Abdullah became Emir of Transjordan (now Jordan) from 1921 to 1946 and King from 1946 (when the country became fully independent) to 1951 when he was assassinated by an Arab fanatic. His son Tallal succeeded him briefly until the late King Hussein came to the throne in 1952, the latter's death on the 5th of February 1999 marking the end of the longest reign of any Middle Eastern monarch. When the French expelled Feisal from Syria he became King of the British mandated territory of Iraq which became independent in 1932. Feisal died in 1933 and was succeeded by his only son Ghazi who was killed in an accident in 1939. Ghazi's son Feisal II, born in 1935, ruled under the aegis of his uncle Abdul Illah until 1958. In the same year Feisal IInd and his cousin King Hussein of Jordan proclaimed a federation of their two kingdoms and this was followed almost immediately by a revolutionary coup d'etat led by Brigadier Kassem in which both Feisal and his prime minister Nuri es-Said were murdered. Zeid, the Sherif's youngest son whose mother was Turkish, had no great interest in Arab Independence. He lived for many years in London and died in 1961.

Chapter **21**

JOHN BRUCE'S STORY

In 1968 an article appeared in the 'Sunday Times' newspaper entitled 'How Lawrence of Arabia cracked up', by Colin Simpson and Phillip Knightly. In it they described how a Mr John Bruce approached the newspaper 'explaining that he had refused to talk before because he had promised Mrs Bernard Shaw that he would keep Lawrence's secret while Lawrence's mother Sarah was alive' - the latter had died nine years earlier on 16th November 1959.

The newspaper men checked Bruce's credentials and confirmed that Lawrence a) had been in the Tank Corps at the same time as Bruce, b) was godfather to Bruce's son, c) had made Bruce's mother Mary an allowance from his R.A.F. pay and d) had described Bruce in a letter to Mrs Shaw.' (In fact a small allocation was made out of book royalties from one of the Lawrence trusts not only to Bruce's mother but also to Bruce's son).

Lawrence met Bruce in the Spring of 1922 when the Scotsman came south to London looking for a job with a firm of merchant bankers owned by a friend of his, Francis Rodd. For some reason, Lawrence was present at Bruce's interview with Rodd and although Bruce was not appointed,

Lawrence arranged to see him the following Friday, which entailed Bruce having to travel back from his home in Aberdeen. According to Bruce, Lawrence told him that 'he was a Colonel in the army with a responsible job but that he was in grave financial difficulties and might have to submit to some unpleasant things. What he needed was someone discreet, strong and alert who would do as he was told without question and who could be trusted with highly confidential personal matters ...' Bruce accepted Lawrence's offer, was put on a three month trial at a salary of £3 a week and sent back to Aberdeen to await instructions.

By the 17th of August 1922, which was when Sir Hugh Trenchard, Chief of the Air Staff, finally acceded to Lawrence's persistent requests and signed an authority for him to join the Royal Air Force, Lawrence, say Simpson and Knightly, 'was emotionally exhausted and financially embarrassed. His Colonial Office salary of £1,200 a year had ceased and his commitments totalled nearly £7,000. He was now spending his time writing 'Seven Pillars' in an attic at No. 14 Barton Street whilst Bruce, now returned from Aberdeen, lodged at the Union Jack Club. The £3 a week salary from Lawrence had stopped, but Bruce took on jobs and picked up what money he could'.

At his Barton Street attic, Lawrence related to Bruce 'his family background, dwelling on his illegitimacy, of the difficulties of his being a public figure - and, more mysteriously, of the strain of waiting for some member of his father's family to denounce him. He told Bruce of the debts he had incurred, the money he had given away (to his friends, out of charity) and the pressure that his bank had put upon him. There had been, he said, only one solution: to write a book, hope for a good sale, pay his debts and have enough left over to retire to the country and live quietly. But even finding the money to live whilst finishing the book was proving difficult.

'Lawrence further explained to Bruce that his father had died in 1919 (which was true), but instead of inheriting his money, as he expected, the bulk of it had gone to a cousin, a Mr Fetherstonhaugh Frampton, who owned the Moreton estate near Bovington in Dorset. Lawrence said he had gone to see the cousin, explained his predicament, and asked him to stand as his guarantor. He 'thereafter referred to Frampton as 'The Old Man'.

❧

The 'Old Man' story was not without a grain of truth in it because Lawrence did in fact have distant relatives in nearby Moreton, who were unenthusiastic about acknowledging the Lawrence family on account of the five sons being born out of wedlock. The connection arose by virtue of the marriage of Lawrence's paternal great-uncle Sir Benjamin Chapman to Maria, sister of Henry Rupert Fetherstonhaugh Frampton who lived at the manor of Moreton where he was the local squire. Henry's father Rupert had married the heiress to lands in Dorsetshire which had been owned by the Frampton family since the 14th century, and this is when the name 'Frampton' was added to his own. The Framptons derived from Westmeath in Ireland - the same county which had nurtured the Chapmans - and Bovington (purchased by the War Office in 1899) had been part of the Dorsetshire estates which they owned.

'At first Lawrence said The Old Man had received him civilly enough and had agreed to help him, but had then changed his mind. The Old Man, Lawrence said, had been furious because Lawrence had insulted King George V by declining to receive his decorations awarded him during the war...' Bearing in mind that it was Winston Churchill who originally admonished him for snubbing the King, this authority figure was perhaps in Lawrence's mind an amalgam of the former person and the camp commandant at Bovington who was also referred to as 'The Old Man'.

'Lawrence indicated to Bruce that because of this and other incidents the Old Man had revoked his agreement to help, and would only change his mind if he, Lawrence, 'was prepared to accept harsher terms'.

'The terms were strange, said Lawrence. Not only was he to assign the copyright of his book 'Seven Pillars' to the Old Man, but he was to cut himself off from society. He was to abandon his connections with the prominent people he had met during the war. He was (according to the Old Man) a disgrace to the decent half of his family. Henceforth he would do as he was told, or the Old Man would expose him and his illegitimacy'.

'The Old Man's plan for the isolation of Lawrence was stranger still. Lawrence (having by this time been forced to leave the R.A.F.) was to enlist under an assumed name in the Tank Corps... Every month Lawrence was to make a report on his activities and general behaviour. The Old Man would then decide what punishment or reward was merited and Lawrence was to accept this without question. Punishment might include corporal punishment. The concerned Bruce then decided to return to Aberdeen, but Lawrence made him promise to return if sent for.

'Now desperately short of money, Lawrence was forced to 'sleep occasionally on benches in Paddington Station or at Salvation Army hostels.' In the wintertime he 'dossed down on a makeshift bed on the pipes at the boiler room of the printers (of his book)'.

'At last the despairing Lawrence wrote to John Bruce in Aberdeen. The young man came south and took a job as chucker out in a Paddington club'. According to Bruce, Lawrence turned up outside the club one night 'dirty, feverish and crying like a baby. I carried him to my digs, bathed him, put him to bed and sat with him listening to his troubles.'

'By the end of February 1923, when Lawrence was somewhat recovered, 'he told Bruce that the Old Man was still on his trail and insisting that he join the Tank Corps. Bruce offered to join with him provided he could be discharged at any time if the life proved unbearable; and Lawrence agreed to arrange it.

'On March 12, under the name of T.E. Shaw, Lawrence enlisted at Bovington and Bruce at Aberdeen.' They entered the Camp together and 'were allocated to B Company, Hut 12. After the usual sixteen weeks basic training he (Lawrence) was posted as Quartermaster's Storeman.'

'In November 1923 Bruce was asked by Lawrence to go and see him. He found him nervous and restive, and Lawrence disclosed a further instalment of his relationship with the Old Man. He was in disgrace again. He had failed to attend Church parades. He had been a disappointment in many ways. Bruce says 'Lawrence said the Old Man had decided he must be punished, and the sentence was to be twelve strokes of the birch. He handed me an unsigned, typed letter which he said was from the Old Man. It was on blue paper. It said that a birch had been dispatched to a nearby station and I was to administer the punishment. Afterwards I was to report in writing if I had done so, and I was to describe Lawrence's behaviour and demeanour under punishment'.

Despite having severe misgivings, Bruce 'collected the birch and thrashed Lawrence the same afternoon.'

However this was not the end of the matter. 'He (Lawrence) went to see him (the Old Man) the same afternoon. The Old Man said it had not been hard enough and it was to be done again. I put rugs over him and left only the area to be beaten exposed. After I had given him twelve he said 'better give me another one for luck.' He went straight off to see the Old Man again and came back with his thumbs up. He said 'That's done the trick.' Later Lawrence gave me an envelope with money in it. He said it was from the Old Man. I can't remember how much. A few quid. I shared it with Lawrence'.

Describing how Lawrence behaved under the punishment, Bruce said 'He just lay there, gritted his teeth and took it. He was as tough as a rail really.' What Bruce did not know, and what Lawrence never told him, was that this first beating occurred on the anniversary of Deraa, which was the night spent with the Turkish Bey'.

'Over the next twelve years, always around about the anniversary of the Deraa incident (though some have disputed this), Lawrence arranged to have himself beaten. It was a brutal therapy and the men involved in inflicting it - there were others and predecessors of Bruce - are emphatic that it was in the nature of a punishment which Lawrence apparently felt he needed'.

'There is no doubt that Lawrence continued in a state of deep emotional depression. About Christmas 1925, for example, Bruce - at Clouds Hill for the week-end - became so concerned that he secretly checked on Lawrence's revolver. 'I knew there was a revolver in the box room opposite to where we were. Also kept there were the sleeping bags. As the evening wore on I said I would get the bags ready. I went to get them and at the same time I looked to see if the gun was still there. It was, but loaded. I took the bullets out, and took the box with the rest of them, put the gun back and the cartridges I put in my sleeping bag'.

When Lawrence went outside to the lavatory, Bruce looked in the chest and the gun had gone. 'I took six cartridges and went down to the door... In the still of the night I heard a click. When he (Lawrence) did get to the door I asked if he had been looking for something, He said 'No.' I asked 'Not even these?' holding out the cartridges in my hand and in the half light I could see his eyes popping out of his head. Then he said 'Give them to me' and tried to snatch them from me. 'No you give me that right now,' I said and a little scuffle took place, he trying to get the cartridges and me trying to get the gun. I bashed his hand against the wall until he dropped it, then he cried like a child. I got him up the stairs but I'm afraid there was no sleep that night. There is no doubt he was ending it (i.e. intending to take his own life), because the next day we destroyed eighteen letters which he had written to various people before I arrived'.

Corroboration of Bruce's story comes from another service companion whose role it was to witness the beatings by Bruce. Professor John E. Mack, in his book 'A Prince of our Disorder', writes 'The companion observed three beatings with a metal whip between 1931 and 1934. They were brutal, delivered on the bare buttocks, and a precise number of lashes were required. Lawrence submitted to them 'like a schoolboy', registered obvious fear and agony, but did not scream or cry out. He required that the beatings be severe enough to produce a seminal emission'.

Chapter 22

'RAPE TRAUMA SYNDROME'

Churchill, who in July 1922 finally and reluctantly agreed to Lawrence's discharge from the Colonial Office, admitted to a feeling of sadness when the latter left the scene, and hazarded a guess at his reasons for doing so. '... I am sure' wrote Churchill 'that the ordeal of watching the helplessness of his Arab friends to whom he had pledged his word, and as he conceived it the word of Britain, treated in this manner, must have been the main cause which decided his eventual renunciation of all power in great affairs'.

Yes, Lawrence undoubtedly felt he had let the Arabs down, but was this sufficient reason for him to disregard the opportunities offered to him by Churchill and instead chose to live in relative obscurity after having accomplished such great things? Lawrence described Churchill as 'a great man... for whom I have not merely admiration, but a very great liking. If we get out of the Middle East Mandates with credit, it will be by Winston's bridge'. And in 1927, Lawrence described 'the settlement which Winston put through in 1921 and 1922' as 'the best possible settlement which Great Britain, alone, could achieve at the time'. 'After June 1922 my job was done. I had repaired, so far as it lay in English power to repair it, the damage done to the Arab Movement by the signing of the Armistice in Nov. 1918'. In other words Lawrence by that time was reasonably satisfied with the outcome of events. Were there other more compelling reasons for Lawrence's lack of ambition? For instance, could the death of Dahoum have been a factor?

'I loved you, so I drew these tides of men into my hands
and wrote my will across the sky in stars
To earn you Freedom, the seven pillared worthy house,
that your eyes might be shining for me
When we came'

With this poem, adapted by his friend the poet Robert Graves, Lawrence commenced his 'Seven Pillars of Wisdom' - the title being drawn from the Book of Proverbs, 'Wisdom hath builded a house: she hath hewn out her seven pillars' - of which he wrote the greater part between the February and June of 1919.

This poem was dedicated to one 'S.A.', whose identity was for so long a mystery but is now known with some certainty.

Of the deep friendship between Lawrence and Dahoum there is no doubt, and it is reflected in a letter the former wrote to R.A.M. Guy of the R.A.F. in December 1923. 'People aren't friends till they have said all they can say, and are able to sit together, at work or rest, hour-long without speaking. We never got quite to that, but were nearer it daily... and since S.A. died I haven't experienced any risk of that happening.'

The identity of the mysterious 'S.A.' is discussed in an article by Colin Simpson and Phillip Knightly in the 'Sunday Times Weekly Review' of the 16th of June 1968. Rough notes which Lawrence made in 1919 for the dedicatory poem include the words 'I wrought for him freedom to lighten his sad eyes: but he had died waiting for me. So I threw my gift away and now not anywhere will I find rest and peace', from which Simpson and Knightly deduce that 'S.A.' was a man and that whoever he was, he died before 1919.

The two authors then refer to an episode from 'Seven Pillars' which was omitted for security reasons. 'Lawrence made a trip through Turkish lines to enemy-occupied Damascus to try to persuade eminent Arabs to rise up against the Turks at the right moment. Even today (1968) the tortured politics of Syria surround this trip with secrecy, yet the Wingate (Sir Reginald) papers in Durham University reveal a recommendation that Lawrence receive the V.C. for it. Wingate appends a note saying that though the recommendation ostensibly refers to Lawrence's bravery at the capture of Akaba it was in reality a recognition of the Damascus trip, adding that security demanded that until further notice the fact should be concealed.' 'In Damascus Lawrence went to see an Arab Sheik who was there on his behalf, only to find him dead or dying of Typhus.'

(The word 'Sheik', meaning 'Arab ruler' is misleading, given the lowly status of Dahoum, though it may have been used in jest by his friends. However it is clear that the 'Ahmed' referred to by the authors is Selim Ahmed, or 'Dahoum' and this, to their mind, 'is the only person who fits all the clues'. In fact Dahoum died in September 1918, only one month before the Allies entered the city.

We have further corroboration of the truth of this view from the poet and novelist Robert Graves, who said that Lawrence had told him personally that 'S.A.' was Ahmed.

Lawrence's grief at the death of Dahoum was akin to that of a father who has lost his son. Into Dahoum's hands, and into those of all the Arabs, he had dreamed of placing the gift of Arab independence and self-determination, and now the boy had died before it had been achieved. Lawrence had thrown his gift away, or in other words left Dahoum in Damascus instead of keeping him by his side, and now he was inconsolable.

So yes, the death of Dahoum may have been a factor in Lawrence's about-turn. Also the fact that he Lawrence was exhausted, as he himself admitted. 'If ever there was a man squeezed right out and dry by over-experience' he wrote to Herbert Baker (the young architect whom Lawrence had met in Oxford and who had given him the use of a room above his London office in Barton Street, Westminster in which to write his book 'Seven Pillars' in peace) in 1922 'then it's me.

I refuse to say 'ever' or 'never' of myself, or anything alive: but I don't think that I'll ever be fit for anything again'.

However against this must be weighed Lawrence's powers of endurance and stamina which were legendary, and there is no doubt that given a period of respite he would in the normal course of events have recovered. A.G. Prys-Jones, who was in the year below him at Jesus College, Oxford wrote 'He (Lawrence) never seemed to be able to get his puttees wound correctly, and the hang of his uniform showed considerable eccentricity'. Also that he preferred to take his slumber outside rather than inside the tent, but was an excellent marksman and showed no exhaustion after any route march.

Might there not however be another factor which, unlike disillusionment, bereavement or exhaustion, the passage of time actually made worse rather than better - which brings us to the rape episode. Some have questioned whether this episode at Deraa was a figment of Lawrence's imagination. This is unlikely, a doctor having subsequently noticed on his back the marks of the flogging, which were still present some five years later.

❦

'Rape trauma syndrome' as it is called, may leave the victim with a variety of feelings which were described by S.S. Ageton in 1983. Immediately after the assault there may be embarrassment, depression and guilt. Over the following two years these feelings reduce substantially, especially in the first year, but after two years the feeling are substantially increased, particularly the depression. In fact Lawrence became extremely depressed and actually contemplated suicide. Ageton also describes an increased fear in the victim of being alone.

If Lawrence was indeed suffering the chronic and progressively worsening symptoms of 'Rape Trauma Syndrome', then this helps to explain his lack of motivation. But how do we explain his desire to be punished?

Richie J. McMullen, in his book 'Male Rape', states that 'For some male victims, rape might constitute their first ever sexual experience' and this certainly appears to have been the case with Lawrence. He goes on to describe a scenario which might well fit Lawrence. 'So guilty do they (the victims of rape) feel about being aroused the first time and then going along with things, especially if the sexual content of the rape matches up to a previous inner fantasy ... that they are in real danger of leaning towards a self-constructed passive sexuality. That is, the association made between sexual arousal and being abused and raped may lead them into adopting a masochistic sexual lifestyle'.

It seems likely that from the time he was raped onwards, Lawrence associated beating with sexual arousal and actively sought out someone who would beat him. The question is, was this self-prescribed 'treatment' designed to subdue his sexual feelings, or to reinforce them?

One clearly identified reaction in rape victims, says McMullen, is fear. This can be so great as to cause a 'physiological reaction within the victim whereby he becomes sexually aroused, and it can have serious consequences long after the rape event'. There may also be bad dreams and nightmares - which we know Lawrence also suffered from. A.C. Kinsey has also reported that boys frightened by the emotional fear of punishment may respond physiologically by experiencing sexual excitation including erection and ejaculation.

McMullen states that if in the process of being raped the victim ejaculates, he may in consequence be 'bewildered by his physiological response to the offence' and fear that he himself actually is homosexual just as he assumes his attacker to be. Thereafter the victim, if he is heterosexual, may 'find it difficult to maintain or establish sexual relations with members of the opposite sex' and may also 'question their masculinity and doubt their manhood'.

The victim will afterwards almost invariably blame himself for what happened, even if to do so 'makes no objective sense'. He may convince himself that he gave his consent because, during the rape, he became sexually aroused and had an erection or had an orgasm. He confuses sexual arousal with consent and assumes that 'penile erection is within conscious control', which it is not.

We might also enquire as to what this 'previous inner fantasy' described by McMullen might have been. Two possibilities spring to mind as to their origin. Firstly the beatings administered by his mother as a child - it is known that some men are sexually aroused by being beaten by women, a famous example being the philosopher Henri Rousseau who gives a first hand account of such a happening in his book 'Confessions' - and this may be why Lawrence described his mother as being 'very exciting'. Secondly Lawrence in reading accounts of mediaeval chivalry would have been familiar with the idea of flagellation, the scourging of the body in penance for the sins of the world. His brother Arnold firmly believed that Lawrence's '...subjection of the body was achieved by methods advocated by the saints whose lives he had read' - to quote his own words. By being beaten, Lawrence may have hoped to be emotionally 'cleansed' in the same way that when a person has been raped, they will try to scrub themselves clean. If this was the case, then it may have confused Lawrence that instead of subduing his erotic desires, the beatings reinforced them to the point of ejaculation.

Other factors which may have driven Lawrence to seek out this punishment were feelings of unworthiness resulting from his illegitimacy, and guilt about his perceived surrender to the rape at Deraa.

And what of John Bruce's role in all of this? His genuine concern for Lawrence manifested itself not only in the way he intervened in the suicide attempt but also by his protection of the latter from those fellow servicemen in the hut who, taking advantage of Lawrence's good nature, tried to borrow money from him. Far from deriving pleasure from beating Lawrence, Bruce shows his distaste when he says 'It is nasty. The prongs (of the birch) go into the skin and break the blood vessels and it bleeds'.

⋘⋙

Lawrence's need to introduce the fictional story of the 'Old Man' as the person who was driving the events may be explained by the idea of 'Transactional Analysis' introduced by Dr Eric Berne, an American psychiatrist in the early 1960s. Berne proposed that every human being has three ego states - a 'parent', an 'adult' and a 'child' - each with its own way of thinking, feeling and behaving, and during the course of each day he or she will spend some time in each state. He describes how the rules and moral dictums provided by our parents in early life influence us in the years to come. If our parents were strict and rigid, then 'the parent' we have inside of us may be equally strict and unforgiving and 'the parent's' words full of commands and value-judgments - which in Lawrence's case is personified in the shape of the 'Old Man'.

Therefore the 'Old Man' was one of Lawrence's alter egos - the parent that is within us all. Although in childhood it had been his mother who administered the discipline, he was perhaps trying to recreate her influence but preferred a male role-model which he felt happier with as it did not involve heterosexual feelings. And so by substituting the 'Old Man' for the negative aspect of his mother's personality, Lawrence became locked into a repetitive and destructive 'transaction'.

It is by seeing Lawrence as a victim of 'Rape Trauma Syndrome' that we gain some understanding of the pattern of his subsequent behaviour. 'Being a victim (of rape)' states McMullen ' means being powerless. It means not being able to control or direct one's body, life or circumstances. It means lacking autonomy and the freedom to self-govern or self-regulate. It also means not having the power of self-determination...'

And so we see Lawrence content to live thereafter in relative obscurity in the lower ranks of the armed services, where others would provide his meals, make decisions for him and in short absolve him of having to take any responsibility for his own life.

Chapter 23

SIR HUGH TRENCHARD AND THE R.A.F.

Born in 1873 Hugh Montague Trenchard was a colonel in the Royal Scots Fusiliers and had fought in South Africa before joining the Royal Flying Corps. During the Great War he commanded the British air forces in France and promoted the idea of an independent air force and the notion of strategic bombing. He was chief of the air staff from 1918 to 1929 and became the first marshal of the R.A.F. in 1927.

In January 1922 Lawrence wrote to Trenchard, whom he had met at the Cairo Conference where the latter had been present as representative of the Royal Air Force, saying he would like to join the R.A.F. 'in the ranks, of course'. Lawrence was aged 33 and in good health and the reason put forward was that he wanted to write another book. 'I see the sort of subject I need in the beginning of your Force' he said, and admitted that it was an 'odd request'.

In the July of 1922 after Churchill had agreed to release him, Lawrence was invited to Trenchard's home at Barnet where the latter tried without success to persuade him to accept a more responsible position. And so on 30th August 1922 Lawrence was allowed to join the R.A.F. as '352087

Aircraftsman John Hume Ross'. Here, during basic training at Uxbridge and later at the R.A.F. School of Photography at Farnborough, he gained the material to write his second literary work 'The Mint'

He gave his reasons for enlisting in a letter to Dr Hogarth of 13th June 1923. 'The security of it first; seven years existence guaranteed. I haven't any longer the mind to fight for sustenance. As you realise I've finished with the 'Lawrence' episode. I don't like what rumour makes of him - not the man I'd like to be! and the life of politics wearies me out, by worrying me over-much. I've not got a coarse-fibred enough nature for them, and have too many scruples and an uneasy conscience...'

However in December the Daily Express newspaper revealed on its front page the identity of this 'Famous War Hero' and as a consequence in March 1923 Lawrence was forced to transfer to the Army.

John Bruce, 1923.
Courtesy John Bruce.

Lord Trenchard
Courtesy of ational Portrait Gallery, London

Chapter 24

BOVINGTON CAMP AND CLOUDS HILL

In March 1923 Lawrence is to be found as a private soldier in the Tank Corps Training School at Bovington, Dorset under a new alias 'T.E. Shaw', a name he may have borrowed from George Bernard Shaw whose plays he admired. The following spring he writes again to Trenchard saying his main reason for staying in the Army is 'the hope of getting back into the R.A.F.'

≈≈≈

It was in the September of 1923 whilst motorcycling back to Bovington from Thomas Hardy's house at Max Gate, Dorchester, that Lawrence stopped at a small derelict cottage set amongst rhododendrons down a narrow track. 'Clouds Hill' as it was called was owned by a cousin of his from whom he agreed to rent it for the sum of half a crown per week. At this time Eric Kennington, who Lawrence had commissioned amongst others to illustrate 'Seven Pillars', noticed a deterioration in the latter's condition in that he seemed 'possessed of devils, visibly thinner, pale, scarred and savage.' There is no doubt that he was depressed. He also suffered recurrent bouts of malaria caught as a child when in Paris.

On the architrave above the front door Lawrence carved the words 'OU OPOVTIS'. This derives from a tale told about Hippocleides by the Greek historian Herodotus and means 'Does not care', or in Lawrence's words '… nothing in Clouds Hill is to be a care upon its habitant. While I have it there shall be nothing exquisite or unique in it. Nothing to anchor me'.

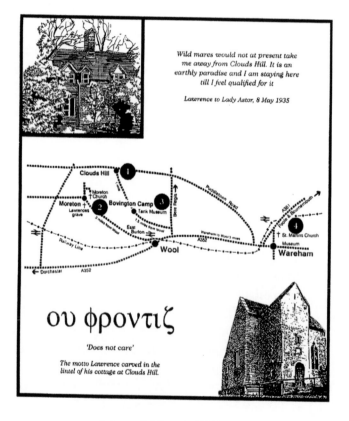

Wild mares would not at present take me away from Clouds Hill. It is an earthly paradise and I am staying here till I feel qualified for it

Lawrence to Lady Astor, 8 May 1935

ου φροντιζ

'Does not care'

The motto Lawrence carved in the lintel of his cottage at Clouds Hill.

Map of Clouds Hill.

Chapter 25

RETURN TO THE R.A.F.

Two years later in February 1925 Lawrence is desperate and writes to Trenchard 'Have I no chance of re-enlistment in the R.A.F., or transfer?' and begs him not to turn him down again 'just because you did so last year and the year before'.

Much as he disliked army life, however, it was not until August 1925 that he was allowed, after representations to Prime Minister Stanley Baldwin by Bernard Shaw and John Buchan, author and Director of Intelligence at the Ministry of Information, to return to the R.A.F. Enrolled as 'Ordinary Aircraftsman Shaw', he was sent first to the Cadet College at Cranwell in Lincolnshire and was to remain in the service until his retirement in 1935. Prior to his reinstatement Lawrence, whilst staying with Trenchard, had threatened to take his own life, whereupon the latter, who in reality was attached to him and worried greatly over his welfare, made a joke of it and said 'All right, but please go into the garden. I don't want my carpets ruined'.

However six months later in January 1927 we find him in India, having told Trenchard that 'neither good-will on the part of those above me, nor correct behaviour on my part can prevent my being a nuisance in any camp where the daily press can get at me'. He had requested this posting the previous year as he was anxious to avoid the inevitable publicity which he knew would ensue with the publication of Jonathan Cape's unlimited edition of 'Seven Pillars'.

From Drigh Road Air Station near Karachi (now Pakistan) he wrote to Trenchard to tell him about 'The Mint', a notebook of 170 pages, a 'worm's eye view of the R.A.F. - a scrappy uncomfortable thing' and so-called 'because we were all being stamped after your (i.e. Trenchard's) image and superscription'. Lawrence admitted that 'The general public might be puzzled, and think I didn't like the R.A.F.' whereas in fact he found it 'the only life worth living for its own sake'.

In August 1927 Lawrence makes his change of name to 'Shaw' official by Deed Poll and two months later is promoted by reason of his length of service to Aircraftsman Grade 1 from Grade 2.

In July 1928 Trenchard, who had read 'The Mint', writes to Lawrence expressing concern that the book might be misunderstood and therefore damage the R.A.F. if its contents were to be made public. Trenchard, not unsympathetic to Lawrence's views, was aware of certain shortcomings in the service and that there were reforms to it which he wished to make. His aim was also to develop air power to be a means of preventing unnecessary killings and casualties in war.

Lawrence, having seen R.A.F. life 'from the ground', as he put it, also suggested reforms to the way in which the service was run, some of which were implemented whilst he was a serving aircraftsman and others after he left. Amongst them were the abolition of compulsory church parades and the progressive step of ensuring that, where possible, servicemen were posted to stations near their homes. Also the elimination of swagger sticks, permission to leave the service voluntarily and the abolition of the death penalty for desertion and cowardice in the face of the enemy.

On December 21st 1928 Lawrence writes to Trenchard about the latter's resignation from the R.A.F., describing him as the father of the service, the one who in ten years created it 'from the ground up'. On the 27th he writes again and, notwithstanding his lowly position as aircraftsman, couches his letter in familiar terms. 'I'm a believer in the parent bird getting out, when the chick's done his first solo', he says, and compares his chief's action with his own when he got 'right out of the Arab business, so soon as it seemed a going concern. Arab nationality was as much my creation as the R.A.F. was yours'.

❧

Unfortunately for Lawrence, on January 8th 1929 after only two years in India, the authorities were obliged to send him back to England from his second posting at Miranshah in the northwest of India following rumours in the press that he was actively involved in the rebellion in nearby

Afghanistan, whose border was a mere ten miles away.

Chapter 26

'THE MINT'

When in August 1922 he joined the R.A.F. under the name of 'John Hume Ross', and three years later in 1925 when he re-enlisted after a spell in the army at Bovington, Lawrence made the notes which were to be the basis of his book about the service which he called 'The Mint'. It is from this book that we glean an insight into the state of his mind at this period of his life.

At first he is in a state of panic and describes 'the melting of the bowels before a crisis', and his nerves which were 'like a rabbit'. When the doctor notices the scars on his back caused by the attentions of the attendants of the Turkish Bey at Deraa, Lawrence dismisses them as 'superficial wounds'. '... since April I've been taking off my friends what meals I dared' he states, and hopes in vain that the doctor will not notice how thin he is. However he is relieved to think it will be 'Seven years now before I think of winning a meal' - or in other words not have to worry about where the next meal is coming from.

He lies 'sickly' on his 'allotted bed', his bedfellow 'perfect fear', and as the men indulge in horseplay he wonders 'how we (as new recruits) should bear the freedom of this fellowship'. He thinks living might be worse than death. 'Only for survivors is there an after-pain'. Upon being required to swear the oath he speaks of an 'unformulated loyalty ... obscurely grown' which he has discovered 'while walking the streets or lanes of our own country', and believes this is an 'ideal' which, unlike the King, 'cannot have legs and a hat'.

'... a man's enlisting is his acknowledgment of defeat by life', says Lawrence. 'Amongst a hundred serving men you will not find one whole and happy'. 'Every man in the hut, bar me, tries shamelessly to sing and hum and whistle' - but why he is the only one not to join in he does not explain.

He curses the stick, the 'slip of black cane with a silver knob' which the men are obliged to carry as they walk, the rule being that it is held 'parallel with the ground', 'the hand going back as the foot went forward', and admits 'that fear is with us when we break that rule'.

We glimpse his shyness and modesty when he conveys 'slyly to the ever-open incinerator' a small picture of himself, which hangs in the canteen alongside those of 'King George, Trenchard, Beatty, Haig, some land-girls' and 'a destroyer at speed'.

And again, when a commendation from the King falls accidentally onto the floor from his notebook, Lawrence hides it from his friend Parker and pretends it is his birth certificate.

It is a point of honour with Lawrence that even when he is exhausted from shovelling 'pig-shit' into a lorry, he does not 'fall down and fail in a job' because 'with my pound-note accent' he believes 'they'd have taken it for granted I was too soft for man's work'.

Lawrence describes his body as being 'unpleasantly taut', and he is prone to accidents such as when he falls on wet tarmac and breaks a little finger, or sprains an instep whilst carrying a sack of flour.

Lawrence's determination to subject himself to the will of those in authority over him, however unpleasant this experience may be, is apparent in his attitude to Corporal Abner. 'We are all ridden beasts; and of our officers and N.C.O.s some will be bad riders. We must acquire the stolidity to carry on and like the work too well to let it suffer, however they mishandle or punish us, ignorantly. The R.A.F. is bigger than itself'. He suspects Abner of 'resenting much that he had to make us undergo, and of seeing the futility of most routine' and observes 'Routine is too often an easy way of saving thought'.

Lawrence's hatred of bullying is revealed when he describes Corporal Raper, 'who assumed great licence in the camp' because he had won the V.C., 'degrading himself and his species' by making one of the men, Clarke, who had taken off his boot to remove a nail, run up and down the alley of the hut with one boot off and the other on.

Lawrence's support for the underdog had previously manifested itself in his support for the

Arabs in their struggle against Turkish domination. This was notwithstanding the fact that the former were of the Muslim faith, whereas England was nominally Christian as were the mediaeval knights who were his heroes and who had fought against the Turks 900 years before in the Crusades. Now however, when he finds himself having to witness his Commandant humiliating one of the men by flinging the latter's cap to the ground, his emotions almost explode. 'I found myself trembling with clenched fists, repeating to myself, 'I must hit him, I must,' and the next moment trying not to cry for shame that an officer should play the public cad'.

Sergeant Pearson he describes as 'our worst tormentor'. At question time 'he made a fool of me, as is too easy for an instructor with a stammering recruit. Some sense of discipline ties me, tongue-ties me'. However despite the sergeant's foul and hurtful names 'I hung there, more curiously miserable than indignant'. Lawrence's failure to look the sergeant in the eye inflames the latter even more. "Look at me!' he yells: but I can't. If I am angry, I can outface a man; but when this hyaena (the sergeant) curses me I sicken with shame wondering if my authority, in the past, so deflowered myself and those under me'.

'Touch' he says 'I fear and shun most, of my senses'. He has never indulged in 'venery' (sexual intercourse) 'never having been tempted so to peril my mortal soul...' - advice given to him years ago at Oxford by the select preacher at evening

service, which demonstrates that Lawrence had by
no means discarded fully the Christian principles
which were instilled into him by his parents. If the
'pleasure' (of the sexual act) 'is indeed no more
than a convulsion' lasting as the preacher was
'credibly informed' for 'less than one and three-
quarter minutes', then 'the temptation flickers out
into the indifference of tired disgust once a blue
moon, when nature compels it'. Lawrence was
therefore no different from other men in that he
had sexual desires, even if they manifested
themselves only infrequently. Speaking of
sodomy, he says 'anyone listening in to a hut of
airmen would think it a den of infamy. Yet we are
too intimate, too bodily soiled, to attract one
another', yet he admits that '... in the four large
camps of my sojourning there have been five
fellows actively beastly. Doubtless their natures
tempted others: but they fight its expression as the
normal airman fights his desire for women, out of
care for physical fitness' - by which he is
presumably referring to the danger of venereal
disease.

Of Lawrence's affection and concern for his
fellow aircraftmen there is no doubt, yet he does
not spare us vivid descriptions of horseplay
between the men and the basic language which is
their stock in trade. 'Nobby is miserable', he
writes. 'We keep him company, afraid that he
wishes to destroy himself. Lofty talks of being
bought out, for he is too physically loose to
control his arms and legs in drill and so is always
under punishment'. And later 'Enter White with

tea and shortcake biscuit for Sailor, who took them, clapped biscuit over cup and inverted it successfully, crying, 'Elementary fucking science".

Later in 'The Mint' he contrasts life at the 'Depot' - 'a savage place' - with his new life at the Cranwell Cadet College, which he describes as 'different' and 'humane'. He is always 'a slow starter, always unfavourably impressed' whenever he is 'dropped into a hut full of strangers', and displays tolerance and also patience when he says it is 'only after their crudities (i.e. the men's) have been well learned and forgiven that the more interesting core appears'. The beds are so hard that the airmen 'sleep very restlessly', constantly shifting, groaning, muttering, dreaming and sometimes saying 'beastlike things in their sleep'.

Gradually, however, we begin to see a happier and more contented Lawrence, who rushes out in breeches, puttees and gauntlets at night after a day's work for a ride on his motorcycle, which he calls 'Boanerges'. Its 'first glad roar at being alive again nightly jarred the huts of Cadet College into life. 'There he goes, the noisy bugger', someone would say enviously in every flight. It is part of an airman's profession to be knowing with engines: and a thoroughbred engine is our undying satisfaction. The camp wore the virtue of my Brough (motorcycle) like a flower in its cap. Tonight Tug and Dusty came to the step of our hut to see me off. 'Running down to Smoke, perhaps?' jeered Dusty; hitting at my regular game London and back for tea on fine Wednesday afternoons'.

❧

'The habit of 'belonging to something or other' induces in us a sense of being part of many things' says Lawrence, and describes himself and the men 'sighing in a happy excess of relaxation' as they lay out in the warm sunshine waiting for a 'kite' to return. When they put on their working dress, 'oil, water, mud, paint, all such hazardous things, are instantly our friends'. And when they dive into the swimming pool, whose 'elastic water fits our bodies closely as a skin: - we belong to that too. Everywhere a relationship: no loneliness any more'.

And he ends 'The Mint' by saying 'I can't write 'Finis' to this book, while I am still serving. I hope, sometimes, that I will never write it' which implies that he wishes this happy state of affairs to continue for ever.

Despite Lawrence's reassurances to Trenchard that he will keep 'The Mint' private until at least 1950, in November 1933 the 'British Legion Journal' printed the last three chapters, the document having been presumably leaked by one of the many people to whom Lawrence loaned it. For this Lawrence 'got into awful trouble with the Air ministry' and feared that he 'may be in civvy street next week because of it'. Fortunately for him this was not to be the case. 'The Mint' was finally published in 1955.

And so at last Lawrence finds in the R.A.F. a kind of contentment, where he is no longer lonely or hungry. He has friends, all of whom he knows by nickname, and is free to go off in his spare time on his beloved motorbike 'Boanerges' (son of thunder). He scotches, once and for all, any notion that he is homosexual yet always, in the background, there lurks that fear that has been present within him since Deraa.

Chapter 27

E.M. FORSTER

Running parallel to Lawrence's service life was another of a totally different nature brought about by his love of literature, music and the arts which led him to seek out and cultivate the eminent practitioners of the day. Such a man was the novelist Edward Morgan Forster. Born in 1879 and educated at Cambridge, Forster lived from 1904 to 1907 mainly in Italy and Greece where he gleaned material for his first two novels 'Where Angels Fear to Tread' and 'The Longest Journey', both of which are about the nature of human relationships.

There followed 'A Room With a View' in 1908 and 'Howards End' in 1910. Before the Great War he was in India, and again in 1921 as secretary to the Maharajah of Dewas. The outcome of this was his final novel, 'A Passage to India'. During the war he served in the Royal Welsh Fusiliers in the trenches in France.

Lawrence first met E.M. Forster in February 1920 at a lunch held for Emir Feisal at a Mayfair hotel, and in February 1924 he wrote to the latter in self-deprecatory terms describing himself as an 'imitator' rather than an active writer.

Lawrence explains how he struggled with the book 'Seven Pillars of Wisdom' for four years 'till I was nearly blind and mad'. He had felt 'profoundly dejected over it all' and 'the failure of it was mainly what broke my nerve and sent me into the R.A.F.' Forster had been lent a copy of 'Seven Pillars' by his and Lawrence's mutual friend the poet Siegfried Sassoon and, for all his self-doubt, Lawrence confessed to having 'a longing to hear what men say of it'.

Lawrence had earned a mere eleven pounds from his writing since 1914 and 'a scruple' had prevented him taking his pay whilst out East and also profits 'on any part of the record of the adventure'. He was grateful to Forster for 'bothering to write to me whole pages about my effort' - i.e. 'Seven Pillars', at a time when the latter was himself endeavouring to finish 'A Passage to India'.

Lawrence tells Forster how much he and fellow private soldiers in the Tank Corps at Bovington (who he was in the habit of inviting to Clouds Hill for rest, relaxation and an introduction to classical music particularly that of Bach, Beethoven and Elgar played on his 'Columbia' gramophone), had gained from Forster's recent visit there and how the latter was always 'extremely welcome, as any stranger is almost, but men who write and draw come nearer to my taste than others'. To be in the army, which is his 'assured bread and butter' was clearly a relief to Lawrence and better than 'a gamble outside'.

Forster describes Clouds Hill as follows. 'In those days the two bottom rooms were full of firewood and lumber. We lived upstairs'. There was a 'leathered covered settee... here we talked, played Beethoven symphonies, ate and drank. We drank water only, or tea - no alcohol ever entered Clouds Hill. We drank out of pretty cups of black pottery. T.E. always laid in a stock of tinned dainties for his guests. There were no fixed hours for meals and no one sat down. To think of Clouds Hill as T.E.'s home is to get the wrong idea of it. It wasn't his home, it was rather his pied-à-terre, the place where his feet touched the earth for a moment, and found rest.'

In June 1925 Lawrence writes to Forster correcting some errors in a book entitled 'With Lawrence in Arabia' by Lowell Thomas, the American official correspondent who had visited Akaba for ten days in 1918. Lawrence points out that 'My family isn't Irish from Galway' but was 'an Elizabethan plantation from Leicester in Meath without a drop of Irish blood in us, ever'. Also that his height was actually 5'5" and his weight ten stone.

However it is from Lawrence's comments on Forster's novel 'Dr Woolacott' which is about homosexuality (Forster was himself a homosexual) that we gain further insight into the former's character. He writes of it to Forster in December 1927, shortly after the death of his one-time mentor Dr Hogarth 'for whom I had long cared very greatly'. 'There is a strange cleansing beauty about the whole piece of writing. So passionate, of course; so indecent, some people might say: but I must confess that it has made me change my point of view'. Referring to the episode in Deraa when he was raped, Lawrence says 'The Turks, as you probably know did it to me, by force: and since then I have gone about whimpering to myself unclean, unclean. Now I don't know. Perhaps there is another side, your side, to the story. I couldn't ever do it, I believe: the impulse strong enough to make me touch another creature has not yet been born in me: but perhaps in surrender to such a figure as your 'Death' there might have been a greater realisation - and therefore a more final destruction - of the body than any loneliness can reach'.

These words of Lawrence's make it clear that he never voluntarily participated in, or desired to participate in, any physical relationship whatsoever, let alone one of a homosexual nature

❧

In August 1928 Lawrence is concerned about his book 'The Mint'. He believes Trenchard 'over-estimates the harm which 'The Mint' would do the R.A.F.' but the main reason he has decided to hold back from publication until the year 1950 is 'the horror the fellows with me in the force would feel at my giving them away' or, in other words, portraying them when they were relaxing and off guard.

Forster's opinion is that 'The Mint is not as great a write as The Seven Pillars, either in colour or form; but it is more new, more startling and more heartening than The Seven Pillars or anything else I've read'.

Lawrence's correspondence with Forster continues to 1929, when he is happily installed at R.A.F. Cattewater at Plymouth in Devon. 'A decent little camp, quiet and easy. Very beautifully placed in Plymouth Sound', and finally in October 1932 when he apologises for being unable to afford to send Forster a copy of his translation of the 'Odyssey' (of Homer) which costs twelve guineas.

Lawrence's gatherings at Clouds Hill, a somewhat spartan little cottage with no electricity and only two decent-sized rooms - one on the ground floor which he used as a bedroom-cum-library and the other on the first floor which served as a music room-cum-sitting room - demonstrate one of the most engaging features of his personality - that despite his relative poverty he could enjoy the company of and share cultural experiences with all manner of people from whatever station in life.

Lawrence as Aircraftsman Shaw in his second
R.A.F. period.
Courtesy of the Bodleian Library, University of
Oxford

Edward Morgan Forster, by Dora Carrington
c.1925.
Courtesy of National Portrait Gallery, London

Chapter **28**

GEORGE BERNARD SHAW

Another friend of Lawrence was George Bernard Shaw, who was born in Ireland in 1856, moved to London in 1876, became a socialist and was one of the first to join the socialist Fabian Society in 1884. He became a music critic and journalist and in the 1890s wrote his 'Plays Pleasant', including 'Arms and the Man' (1894) and 'The Devil's Disciple'. (1896)

Further plays followed, often written by him for famous actors and actresses of the day, including 'Captain Brassbound's Conversion', 'Man and Superman', 'Pygmalion' and 'St Joan'. His often flippant and irreverent style had the purpose of provoking people into making them think. His books included 'The Intelligent Woman's Guide to Socialism and Capitalism', published in 1928.

❧❧

Lawrence first met Shaw in March 1922 having been introduced to him by Sydney Cockerell, Curator of the Fitzwilliam Museum, Cambridge. Ever anxious for literary criticism of his work, Lawrence on the strength of this brief encounter asked Shaw if he would 'read, or try to

read, a book which I have written', in other words
Seven Pillars. Shaw, then aged 67, replied on the
1st of December to the effect that it was a great
book but confessed that though his wife Charlotte
had 'ploughed through it', he had not actually read
it yet. Charlotte, whose marriage to Shaw was
platonic and based on companionship only, shared
with Lawrence an Irish background and like him
she had suffered from being dominated by her
mother throughout her childhood.

Aware that Shaw did not believe he had a
serious purpose in joining the armed services and
staying in the ranks, Lawrence wrote to him in
1923 saying 'People come into the army often, not
because it is brutal and licentious, but because
they haven't done very well in the fight of daily
living, and want to be spared the responsibility of
ordering for themselves their homes and food and
clothes and work... Regard it as an asylum for the
little-spirited'. Shaw, however, who thought the
idea 'a maddening masquerade' was impatient and
said that if he did not know Lawrence better he
might conclude that he was 'a depressed mechanic
oiling up fuselages for profanely abusive pilots'.
When the story of Lawrence's enlistment in the
R.A.F. broke in the press, Shaw wrote 'Like all
heroes and, I must add, all idiots you greatly
exaggerate your power of moulding the universe
to your personal convictions. You have just had a
crushing demonstration of the utter impossibility
of hiding or disguising the monster you have
created... It is useless to protest that Lawrence is
not your real name. That will not save you...

Lawrence may be as great a nuisance to you sometimes as G.B.S. is to me, or as Frankenstein found the man he had manufactured; but you created him, and must put up with him as best you can'.

In May 1923 Shaw met Prime Minister Stanley Baldwin and, referring to Lawrence, told him 'the private soldier business is shocking tomfoolery' and urged Baldwin to provide the latter with a pension. However, although Baldwin left Shaw with the impression that the pension would be granted, it never was. Shaw also failed to understand why Lawrence steadfastly refused the notion of taking any profit from his book 'Seven Pillars'.

In October 1924 Shaw sent Lawrence 'Seven Pillars', which the latter had waited a full year for Shaw to criticise and proof read. 'Confound you and your book,' says Shaw 'you are no more to be trusted with a pen than a child with a torpedo' and he then goes on to give Lawrence a lecture on punctuation and the law of libel, and rewrite the appropriate passages for him 'in terms that were not actionable'.

In 1927 we find Shaw again trying to persuade Prime Minister Baldwin to give Lawrence a pension in return for his past services to the nation, and in the following year Lawrence describes Shaw in a letter sent to his mother from India as 'like a tonic. A most sensible, vigorous old man'.

In April 1928 Shaw writes to Lawrence encouragingly about 'The Mint', saying 'the slightest reticence or self-consciousness about it would be misplaced and unpardonable'. However when Shaw suggests that it be put in a library, Lawrence objects saying 'Libraries like the W.O. (War Office) are open only to the officer-class, whose supremacy is based on their not knowing or caring what the men think and feel'.

In July 1928 we again find Lawrence in introspective mood and feeling inadequate. 'What I have wanted and tried to do has always come off, more or less, except when I was trying to write' he tells Shaw 'and then, despite all the good you have said of my books, I am assured of failure. Not complete failure, perhaps... a relative failure, let's call it'.

In 1929 when Lawrence arrives at his new station, R.A.F. Cattewater, it is on a new Brough motorcycle given to him anonymously by the Shaws which would have cost him 'three years of my pay' had he been able to buy it himself. Shaw however, mindful of Lawrence's many spills, has reservations about it - it was, he said, 'like handing a pistol to a would-be suicide'. Shaw demonstrates his concern for Lawrence when he learns that the latter cannot afford to buy himself an overcoat, and kindly lends him his second one.

When in January 1932 Lawrence sends Shaw a critique of the latter's new play 'Too True to be Good' which is a satire on the military establishment, Shaw responds with gratitude and incorporates into it all of Lawrence's suggestions.

Lawrence's last letter to Shaw is written in January 1935, when Mrs Shaw is recovering from blood-poisoning and the couple are planning a holiday abroad.

❧

The two men have a common interest in writing and are mutually supportive to one another, even though Lawrence is desperate for reassurance and Shaw often has to chide him, though always good naturedly, for his lack of self-belief.

However it is with Shaw's wife Charlotte, that Lawrence is to form his deepest and most meaningful relationship.

Chapter **29**

CHARLOTTE SHAW

Over the twelve year period between January 1923 and January 1935 Lawrence wrote at least three hundred letters to Mrs Charlotte Shaw, the wife of the playwright George Bernard Shaw (G.B.S.) who was 31 years his senior, and it is from these that we gain a further insight into the man, his relationship with Sarah his mother, and the effect on him of the experience at Deraa when he was raped by the attendants of the Turkish Bey.

Authors Colin Simpson and Phillip Knightley, writing in the Sunday Times Weekly Review of June 30th 1968, explain how 'After his wife Charlotte died (in September 1943) Bernard Shaw went through her papers. He read T.E. Lawrence's letters to her and her letters to T.E. Lawrence...' And Shaw was later to tell a friend 'In those few hours reading I found out more about my wife than I had learnt in 40 years of marriage.'

It was the opinion of Simpson and Knightley that 'Charlotte's marriage with G.B.S had, by agreement, been childless, and she now directed on Lawrence all the maternal affection she had suppressed for years'. 'It was Charlotte who first discerned the literary genius of Lawrence, who guided his energy, who encouraged him when he needed it and who, above all, allowed him to unburden himself of the guilt he had carried since Deraa'.

In a letter to Mrs Shaw following his first meeting with her and her husband on March 25th 1922, Lawrence talks about 'nearly burning the whole thing (i.e. 'Seven Pillars') for the third time' and asks 'Is there any style in my writing at all? Anything recognisably individual?' And she, having confessed that she has driven her husband 'almost mad by insisting on reading him special bits when he was deep in something else...' asks Lawrence 'How is it conceivable, imaginable that a man who could write the 'Seven Pillars' can have any doubts about it? If you don't know that it is a great book what is the use of anyone telling you so.' '... it is one of the most amazingly individual documents that has ever been written: there is no 'style' because it is above and beyond anything so silly.'

She advises him that 'Your book must be published as a whole' but suggests he omits mention of 'the Sjambok' and 'such little personal severities'.

Unlike his wife, Shaw was critical of the punctuation in the book, and wrote at length to Lawrence about his use of colons, semi-colons, nominatives and so forth. Charlotte, however, persevered and over a two year period corrected proofs, advised on cuts, and gave general encouragement and it was in recognition of this that Lawrence presented her with the very first copy of 'Seven Pillars'. Charlotte was also to help him with his translations of Adrien le Corbeau's

'Gigantesque', Pierre Custot's 'Sturly' - a novel about life under the sea, Homer's 'Odyssey' and later with his own book 'The Mint'.

In March 1924 Lawrence writes to Mrs Shaw about the trial scene in G.B.S's play 'St. Joan' and compares Joan's plight with his rape at Deraa. 'I was thinking of her (Joan) as a person, not as a moral lesson. The pain meant more to me than her example. You instance my night in Deraa. Well, I'm always afraid of being hurt: and to me, while I live, the force of that night will lie in the agony which broke me, and made me surrender. It's the individual view. You can't share it.

'About that night. I shouldn't tell you, because decent men don't talk about such things. I wanted to put it plain in the book, and wrestled for days with my self-respect... which wouldn't, hasn't, let me. For fear of being hurt, or rather to earn five minutes respite from a pain which drove me mad, I gave away the only possession we are born into the world with - our bodily integrity. It's an unforgivable matter, an irrecoverable position: and its that which has made me forswear decent living, and the exercise of my not-contemptible wits and talents.

'You may call this morbid: but think of the offence, and the intensity of my brooding over it for these years. It will hang about me while I live, and afterwards if our personality survives. Consider wandering among the decent ghosts hereafter, crying 'Unclean unclean!'

'You speak of submissive admirers... but that hurts them and me. I'll write you pictures of the two most concerned some day, and will try to show you how far from an object of admiration I must be to them. And the contrary? Do I admire them? There's not a clean human being into whose shape I would not willingly creep. They may not have been Colonel Lawrence... but I know the reverse of that medal, and hate its false face so utterly that I struggle like a trapped rabbit to be it no longer.

'I dodge G.B.S reading part of 'Joan' to me, partly because he's great and I'm worthless: partly because it's my part to shun pleasures... through lack of dessert. There's expiation to be made: and the weak spirit is only too ready to lunch with you, or to enjoy a book, or to hide a quiet while in a cloud-defended cottage: any alleviation of the necessary penalty of living on.'

✦

And so we have Lawrence manifesting in his letters to Charlotte Shaw two of the classical symptoms of a man who has been raped by another man - overwhelming guilt, and a feeling of uncleanliness.

In the June, Lawrence expounds to Charlotte Shaw his views about sexuality. 'Why if fathers and mothers took thought before bringing children into this misery of a world, only the monsters among them would dare to go through with it. The motive which brings the sexes together is 99% sexual pleasure, and only 1% the desire of children, in men, so far as I can learn. As I told you, I haven't ever been carried away in that sense, so that I'm a bad subject to treat of it. I hate and detest this animal side - and I can't find comfort in your compartmenting up our personalities... I think I'm sorry I was brought into the world. I think I'll be glad when I go: but meanwhile I associate myself with the process in any effort to end or mend it.'

In the August his theme is the social dialogue between himself and his fellow aircraftmen and he describes how 'the Air Force fellows are like Oxford undergraduates in their second term... buds just opening after the restraint of school and home. Their first questioning, their first doubt of an established convention, or law, or practice, opens a floodgate in their minds for if one thing is doubtful all things are doubtful: the world to them has been a concrete, founded, polished thing: and the first crack is portentous.

'So the Farnborough fellows used to come to me... after 'lights out' and sit on the box by my bed, and ask questions about every rule of conduct and experience, and about mind and soul and body: and I, since I was lying on my back, could answer succinctly and with illumination. Those who seek me out down here are the keenest ones, and they have been following up the chase of the great Why themselves...'

In September 1925, writing to Charlotte Shaw from R.A.F. Cranwell, Lawrence says 'I've changed, and the Lawrence who used to go about and be friendly with that sort of people is dead. He's worse than dead. He is a stranger I once knew. From henceforward my way will lie with these fellows here, degrading myself... in the hope that some day I will really feel degraded, be degraded to their level. I long for people to look down upon me and despise me, and I'm too shy to take the filthy steps which would publicly shame me, and put me into their contempt. I want to dirty myself outwardly, so that my person may properly reflect the dirtiness which it conceals... and I shrink from dirtying the outside, while I've eaten, avidly eaten, every filthy morsel which chance threw in my way.'

In June 1926 he explains to Mrs Shaw why he 'backed out of the race'. 'I tried (All Souls and elsewhere) to live with decent people, and couldn't. There is too much liberty up aloft. I was able to avoid others all day long: and there is no goodness in being a recluse. So I wrote myself down a failure, socially: and I believed (I still believe) that I'd failed in my ambition to become an artist, at book writing, by taking thought. Creative work isn't achieved by dint of pains. Consequently rather than be a half and half, a Cherry Garrard (polar explorer) or Stephens (Irish poet) or Stanley Baldwin (Prime Minister), I backed out of the race and sat down amongst people who were not racing. Racing, in these modern and specialised days, is a pursuit limited to thoroughbreds and detached observers sometimes wonder whether these over-tensioned, super-charged delicate creatures are bred really to improve the race, or just give pleasure to men-fanciers.'

In February 1927 he reveals something about his attitude to Christianity which, he says, 'has handicapped itself with a growing proportion of people since (the year) 1600 by apparently assuming (i) that we exist, (ii) that man is the centre of his universe, and (iii) that God is, more or less, analogous to man. When you say 'not proven' to (i), 'impossible' to (ii) and 'ridiculous' to (iii), then you lose patience with a crowd which fusses over details like transubstantiation.'

In April 1927 Lawrence describes the tension which exists between himself and his mother who, 'hears from me about 4 times a year, and banalities only. I would like you, if you agree (it is to take a risk) to see her if she comes to England now that China has closed itself to her (the country was at that time being wracked by civil unrest). Mother is rather wonderful: but very exciting. She is so set, so assured in mind. I think she 'set' many years ago; perhaps before I was born. I have a terror of her knowing anything about my feelings, or convictions, or way of life. If she knew they would be damaged, violated, no longer mine. You see she would not hesitate to understand them: and I do not understand them, and do not want to. Nor has she ever seen any of us growing, because I think she has not grown since we began. She was wholly wrapped up in my father, whom she had carried away jealously from his former life and country, against great odds, and whom she kept as her trophy of power...'

'And now two of my brothers are dead (he refers to Frank and Will who were both killed in the Great War), and Arnie (the youngest) and I have left her, and avoid her as our first rule of existence: while my eldest brother (Montague Robert or 'Bob') is hardly her peer or natural companion. It is a dreadful position for her, and yet I see no alternative. While she remains herself and I remain myself it must happen. In all her letters she tells me she is old and lonely, and loves only us; and she begs us to love her, back again, and points us to Christ, in whom, she says, is the only happiness and truth. Not that she finds happiness, herself.

'Of course I shouldn't tell you all this, but she makes Arnie and me profoundly unhappy. We are so helpless; we feel we would never give any other human being the pain she gives us, by her impossible demands, and yet we give her the pain, because we cannot turn on love to her in our letters, like a water-tap; and Christ to us is not a symbol, but a personality spoiled by the accretions of such believers as herself. If you saw her, you whose mind has not grown into a shell-case, perhaps you could show her the other sides and things of which she does not dream. If only she would be content to loose hold of us.

'One of the real reasons (there are three or four) why I am in the service (R.A.F.) is so that I may live by myself. She has given me a terror of families and inquisitions. And yet you'll understand she is my mother and an extraordinary person. Knowledge of her will prevent my ever making any woman a mother, and the cause of children. I think she suspects this: but she does not know that the inner conflict which makes me a standing civil war, is the inevitable issue of the discordant natures of herself and my father, and the inflammation of strength and weakness which followed the uprooting of their lives and principles. They should not have borne children.'

On May 17th 1927 Charlotte replies with a letter to Lawrence with which he would immediately have empathised. 'I had a perfectly hellish childhood and youth,' she states 'after I got old enough to take things in at all.' 'My mother was middle-class, my father was... gentry. My mother was a terribly strong character. She could not bear opposition: if it was offered she either became quite violent or she cried.' 'She felt (and genuinely) that we none of us loved her enough, or considered her enough, or helped her enough. (she would not be helped, ever) or respected her wishes sufficiently, or cared to spend our time with her.'

And Charlotte's description of her father would also have struck a chord with Lawrence. '... gentle, well-educated. He was a marvel of patience with my mother, which was terribly bad for her.'

In August 1927 Lawrence admits to Mrs Shaw 'I've not written any letters of this sort to anyone else, since I was born. No trust ever existed between my mother and myself. Each of us jealously guarded his or her own individuality, whenever we came together. I always felt she was laying siege to me, and would conquer, if I left a chink unguarded.'

Two months later he writes to her expressing a certain satisfaction over his role in the war. 'I was right to work for Arab self-government through 1919 and 1920: and my methods then, though not beyond criticism, were I think reasonably justifiable. The settlement which Winston Churchill put through in 1921 and 1922 (mainly because my advocacy supplied him with all the technical advice and arguments necessary) was, I think, the best possible settlement which Great Britain, alone, could achieve at the time... And after June 1922 my job was done. I had repaired, so far as it lay in English power to repair it, the damage done to the Arab Movement by the signing of the Armistice in Nov. 1918.'

In March 1928 he writes 'The R.A.F. is now my very own service, and I learn to fit in, slowly: to give up my rights to personality.' And in May 'All this finishing and finishing for ten years without the faintest desire or stirring to begin anything anywhere again. I have no more notes for books in my bag: and no urge to join the boy scouts or the House of Commons. The R.A.F. seems natural somehow, as a way of living: and no other life seems natural: or is it that no energy to attempt any new life remains? Nunc dimittis... if I had a Lord, and he were a decent fellow, he would tell his servant to go to sleep, in reward for having worked 'over-time', and very hard, for forty years: or I think he would. It is what his servant (if profitable) would ask as a reward.'

And in November 1928 'My sympathies, in such shows, are always with the weaker side. That's partly, perhaps, why I was able to help the Arabs whole-heartedly (Was it whole-hearted?

Perhaps: but often I think that it's only in trying to write that my whole heart has ever been engaged: and then not for very long)'.

In April 1929 he tells her 'The flaw is that John Bull has announced that I do no work in camp, but tinker with my motor-bike and translate the 'Odyssey'...'

In March 1930 he says 'My St. Andrews degree trouble (the University had wished to confer an honorary degree upon him) is easily over: Barrie (James Matthew Barrie, playwright and novelist) and Buchan (John Buchan, author and politician) played up and freed me from it. I think the public occasion would have been unbearable. A reaction from publicity, which began in me about 1919 had grown stronger since year by year. I like to see my name in the papers - no: when I see it I get a snatch of horrified interest - and I hate anybody telling me they have seen it.'

He tells Mrs Shaw that she is 'the solitary woman who lets me feel at ease with her, in spite of all the benefits you heap on me. Usually I am a very grudging taker too.'

In August 1933 he has learned that his idol, the composer Edward Elgar, is ill. 'If you see him' he asks Mrs Shaw 'will you present my constant pleasure in his music, whether human rendered or from my box? Nobody who makes sounds gets so inside my defences as he does, with his 2nd Symphony and Violin Concerto. Say if the third Symphony has gone forward from those, it will be a thrill to ever so many of us... I feel more and more, as I grow older, the inclination to throw everything away and live on air. We all allow ourselves to need too much.'

In May 1934, when the Shaws have just returned from a cruise, Lawrence has clearly missed them desperately. 'You will think it queer, but I have been looking and longing for this news to appear in the papers. Your return makes England seem furnished, somehow. I so seldom call: yet my two visits to London while you were away found the place barren: and I came back here sooner than was necessary, just because there seemed no point in wandering about.' and he concludes 'I'm ever so glad you are here.'

In December 1934 he writes from Bridlington, his final R.A.F. posting, 'Next year (the year in which he is due to retire) I am going to have to draw in my ink-horns: for this year I have tried - vainly! - not to spend more than 2/- a week on post. After February my total means will be 25/- a week, and I shall not spend more than three pence weekly upon post; after the first week, when I have to warn people that I am ceasing to write.' He continues '... the Brough purred smoothly, to Royston and Biggleswade and Stamford and Grantham and Bawtry and Goole and Bridlington. Even the rain ceased after a while, and I got in warm and dry. Today I have cleaned the good servant till it shines again. All the last two months it has been stored at Clouds Hill, until I felt that it had almost shared my unhappiness in our separation.' And referring to the Shaws' forthcoming visit to New Zealand which commenced in March 1935, 'I hope you get securely and well on to your (ship) 'Reina del Pacifico', and I hope the cruise is a success. When you come back my great change will have happened. I wonder... I wonder how it will be with me. Twelve years ago I thought that the question of an 'after' to the Service would never happen: the twelve years felt as though they would be enough for me. Yet here I am still strong and trenchant-minded, but with nothing in my hand. I have learnt only the word NO in 46 years. However I suppose myself is my own business and I should not trouble others with it. At least you will find me very different, after this.' And he concludes 'I do hope the voyage is excellent. When you come back, Time will mean nothing to me: Then we can meet and not write.'

Lawrence, in his writings to his friend Mrs Shaw with whom he empathised and in whom he confided, demonstrates the classical symptoms of what is now described as 'Rape Trauma Syndrome', these symptoms coming out with typical severity after a prolonged time-interval. He feels utter shame, and a sense of worthlessness; he feels dirty and despicable in other men's eyes and desires that they perceive him in that light. He also shows a lack of purpose and self-determination, all in stark contrast to the energetic and enthusiastic Lawrence of old. Resentments within him concerning his parents' 'discordant natures' and the 'uprooting of their lives and principles' also resurface and demonstrate the long-lasting traumatic effect this had on him in his formative years. He comes across as an intensely private individual desperate to avoid being sucked dry by his mother's limitless emotional demands, and reveals that her treatment of him has made him forever terrified of ever marrying or having children.

Nevertheless his spirit is not entirely vanquished, in that he finds pleasure in intelligent conversation with his fellows and in music, especially that of Elgar, and when the Shaws go away he finds himself eagerly anticipating their return. And always, shining through like a bright beacon, is his asceticism epitomised by his assertion - 'We all allow ourselves to need too much'.

George Bernard Shaw, by Dame Laura Knight.
1932
Courtesy of National Portrait Gallery, London

Charlotte Shaw, by unknown photographer
c. 1919
Courtesy of National Portrait Gallery, London

Chapter **30**

THOMAS HARDY

The literary figure revered perhaps more than any other by Lawrence was Thomas Hardy, born in 1840 at Higher Bockhampton near Dorchester, Dorset. The son of a stone-mason and amateur musician, Hardy was articled to an architect and spent time as a restorer of churches before writing the first of fourteen novels 'Desperate Remedies' which was published in 1871. This was followed in 1872 by 'Under the Greenwood Tree'.

In 1874, the year he wrote 'Far from the Madding Crowd', he married Emma Louisa Gifford who he had met in Cornwall and in 1885 the couple moved into Max Gate, Dorchester, a house which he had built to his own design. There he wrote 'The Return of the Native' (1878), 'The Mayor of Casterbridge' (1886) and 'The Woodlanders' (1886-7) all of which were set in the West Country, referred to by the author as 'Wessex'. A favourite theme of his was the struggle of human beings against the more powerful forces of nature and the Gods. The couple travelled extensively on the continent and lived for a time in London.

The honesty with which he wrote about male/female relationships, as in 'Tess of the D'Urbervilles' (1891), offended Victorian sensibilities and the further criticism which followed the publication of 'Jude the Obscure' in 1895 decided Hardy to write no more novels apart from his final one 'The Well Beloved' in 1897. Thereafter he devoted himself to writing poetry, over one hundred of which expressed the sorrow and remorse he felt following the death of Emma in 1913. From 1904 to 1908 he engaged himself in a monumental epic-drama which he wrote in blank verse called 'The Dynasts' about the Napoleonic wars. In 1910 he was awarded the Order of Merit.

The year after his wife died Hardy married Florence Emily Dugdale, a published author of children's stories who had previously assisted him with researches and typing work over a number of years.

Lawrence had met the writer Robert Graves, who with Siegfried Sassoon was numbered amongst Thomas Hardy's circle of 'war-poet' friends, at a guest night at All Souls' College, Oxford in November 1919. In March 1923 he wrote to Graves from his London address to ask the latter if he thought 'old Hardy would let me take a look at him?' as he, Lawrence considered Hardy to be '…a proper poet and a fair novelist!' The Hardys' home was only ten miles from where Lawrence was stationed at Bovington.

When the answer came back in the affirmative from Mrs. Hardy, who undertook most of the correspondence at Max Gate and saw it as her duty to protect her elderly and distinguished husband from the unwanted attentions of the outside world, Lawrence wrote directly to her admitting that his seeking out the meeting '... feels rather barefaced. I haven't any qualifications to justify seeing Mr. Hardy: only I'd very much like to. 'The Dynasts' and the other poems are so wholly good to my taste'.

In a letter to the sculptor Eric Kennington, (who Lawrence had met following an exhibition of the former's paintings in London in 1920) Lawrence describes his first meeting with Hardy, who he visited from 'Tank-town' Bovington on the 29th of March 1923. '... it was worth it, and I'm going again, if ever he asks me.' However Lawrence is not uncritical of Hardy's books, of which he writes 'his weakness in character-drawing is a reflection of himself. A very sensitive little man, faded now, with hope yet that mankind will give up warfare. He felt incredibly old to me.' Hardy was in fact 82 years old at the time, but Lawrence underestimated his characters – Gabriel Oak, Bathsheba Everdene, Glym Yeobright, Michael Henchard, Tess D'Uberville, Sergeant Troy, Fanny Robin, Angel Clare, Dick Dewey and countless more whose names are now known not only in Hardy's native land but also throughout the world.

In such esteem did Lawrence hold 'The Dynasts' that he told Mrs. Hardy that there was nothing in English Literature between it and Shakespeare, and a leather-bound copy of it inscribed to 'Colonel Lawrence from Thomas Hardy' was found amongst the books in Lawrence's possession at the time of the latter's death.

For his part Hardy read Lawrence's 'Seven Pillars' and according to a letter from the latter to Dr. Hogarth on August 23rd, made Lawrence 'very proud with what he said of it.' Mrs. Hardy also read the manuscript and although her judgement of was 'kindly' she said she preferred the original 'Oxford' text rather than the 'Cape' (Jonathan Cape the publisher) abridgement.

On the 8th of September Lawrence in a letter to Robert Graves contrasted Hardy – 'so pale, so quiet, so refined into an essence' with (Bovington) camp, which was 'such a hurly-burly'. There is, he says 'an unbelievable dignity and ripeness about Hardy, he is waiting so tranquilly for death, without a desire or ambition left in his spirit, as far as I can feel it, and yet he entertains so many illusions and hopes for the world, things which I, in my disillusioned middle age, feel to be illusory. They used to call this man a pessimist. While really he is full of fancy expectations.

'And the standard of the man! He feels interest in everyone and veneration for no-one. I've not found in him any bowing-down, moral or material or spiritual.'

This quality of Hardy's struck a chord with Lawrence, who behaved in much the same way to his own acquaintances, no matter how high or low. 'Max Gate' says Lawrence, 'is a place apart, and I feel it all the more poignantly for the contrast of life in this squalid camp. It is strange to pass from the noise and thoughtlessness of sergeants' company into a peace so secure that in it not even Mrs. Hardy's tea-cups rattle on the tray, and from a barrack of hollow senseless bustle to the cheerful calm of T. H. (Hardy) thinking aloud about life and two or three of us.'

On the 26th of November 1924, Siegfried Sassoon, E.M. Forster and Thomas and Florence Hardy attended the first production of 'Tess of the D'Ubervilles' at the Dorchester Corn Exchange where the actress Gertrude Bugler played the part of Tess. Hardy himself was not present but joined his wife and guests afterwards.

Parlourmaid Nellie Titterington described how Lawrence's visits transformed the household at Max Gate. 'He had a wonderful sense of humour, at least that is how he looked to me, and I always saw and chatted with him when he came and I opened the door. When he called I always asked as a joke, 'Is it Col. Lawrence, Mr. Shaw or Mr. Ross today?' he would smile and say 'Mr. Shaw today'. In front of us maids Mr. Hardy always referred to Lawrence as Mr. Shaw, and Lawrence always called Mr. Hardy, 'T. H.', when speaking to us or in front of Mr. Hardy. Lawrence would come over from Bovington several times a month to talk to him. Indeed he would never pass through Dorchester without a call and a chat.' Describing Max Gate, Nellie says 'a gloom filled the whole atmosphere. That's why Lawrence's visits were such a joy to me. He brought happiness for a few moments. Just to open the door to him was a pleasure. He also brought pleasure to Mr. Hardy, as did several other of his friends… but apart from these occasions it was a house of noiseless gloom.'

Nellie also recalled Hardy's dog 'Wessex', a Caesar terrier, who she described as a 'terror' and 'a fierce, ugly-tempered beast'. 'No guest (at table) could pick up a spoon or anything dropped without the probability of a nasty nip on the hand by 'Wessex'. (Hardy) could do anything with the dog without any danger, while if the dog was in a good mood, Mrs. Hardy could sometimes pick up a dropped object safely. Col. Lawrence … was the only one who could safely deal with Wessex, he could pick anything up without any ill humour on its part. Wessex was very fond of Colonel Lawrence, who would pat him and speak to him and had a wonderful sense of power over him.'

In January 1927 Lawrence wrote to Mrs. Hardy from India to tell her of the 'delightful privilege' it had been for him to have known her and her husband and to have the freedom of Max Gate and saying how much he looked forward to finding them both there when he came back. He also expressed concern for Hardy's health, the latter being now eight-six years of age. Wessex had died and Lawrence said he hoped the dog had had a 'a peaceful parting' and revealed his humanity with the statement, "The killing of animals just because they are ill or old is not medicine we apply to our own species".'

Lawrence was not to see Hardy again because a year later, on January the 11th 1928 when he was still in India, Hardy died. His heart was buried in the churchyard at Stinsford near Dorchester and the remainder of his body was cremated and buried in Westminster Abbey.

Despite the fact that Lawrence felt he could not be a friend of Hardy's because 'the difference in size and age and performance between us was too overwhelming', and blamed himself for intruding upon his presence and troubling his peace, the former was drawn back to the latter time and again. 'I wish I hadn't gone overseas,' said Lawrence later. 'I was afraid, that last time, that it was the last.'

Chapter **31**

FLORENCE HARDY

Lawrence found Max Gate 'so wonderfully unlike' his 'noisy room (at Bovington) that it is difficult to resist...' In December 1923 he explains why he cannot come to lunch with the Hardys on Christmas Day, the reason being that someone has borrowed his motor-bike without permission 'and left her, ruined, in a ditch'.

Mrs Hardy once confessed to a friend Louise Yearsley that Colonel Lawrence had taken her for a ride on the back of his Brough Superior motorcycle along the Wareham Road. Asked how she had enjoyed it, she replied 'I found speed exhilarating'. It was the manufacturer of the motorcycle George Brough's opinion that he never saw Lawrence 'take a single risk nor put any other rider or driver to the slightest inconvenience'.

The war poet and novelist Siegfried Sassoon, another a visitor to Max Gate, described the scene there. 'Got to Max Gate at 4.45. A motor-bike leaning against some shrubs suggested T.E.L. Sure enough, there he was, grinning genially at me through the window of the sitting-room: back view of T.H. also visible. Loud bark from Wessie (the dog 'Wessex') (tied up on the lawn out of sight). Mrs Hardy very smart, all in white silk, greets us in the hall, and T.H. is close behind her, looking exactly the same, and brisk as ever'. Sassoon records that the conversation was mainly about archaeology and that T.E.L. had 'sold his (Arabian) dagger for £120 to pay for doing up his cottage on Clouds Hill'. After tea they 'all trooped out into the garden to inspect the new half-acre of ground Mrs H. (Hardy) has purchased from the Prince of Wales. On it vegetables are grown and chickens kept. We stood looking at the chickens for some time, while Wessie barked at them'.

'She (Mrs Hardy) says she would like a small car' says Sassoon 'but T.H. is very firm against it. His (Hardy's) younger brother (aged seventy-two and stone-deaf) has lately scandalised his parish by purchasing an expensive Sunbeam which he drives furiously'.

In a letter to Mrs Hardy in August 1925, Lawrence explains with regret that his move from Bovington to the R.A.F. Cadet College at Cranwell, Lincolnshire had happened so suddenly was so sudden that there was no time for farewells. Nevertheless he shows he still thinks affectionately of his cottage and his friends when he says 'Alas for Clouds Hill, and the Heath, and the people I had learned in the two years of Dorset'. He asks to be remembered to 'Mr Hardy, who is no doubt wholly taken up now in Tess'. (in other words a dramatised version of his novel).

In November he writes to Mrs Hardy 'Please give Mr Hardy my very best regards. I've promised myself to call as soon as I have the chance. It's a solidity, to be sure that he will be in Max Gate whenever I can come'.

❧

It was whilst Lawrence was with the R.A.F. in Karachi, lying on his bed and listening to Beethoven's last quartet being played on a gramophone, that news came to him of Thomas Hardy's death. To Mrs Hardy he expressed his sorrow and wrote 'It was only you who kept him alive all these years: you to whom I, amongst so many others, owed the privilege of having known him'. And when she wrote back to Lawrence it was to pay the latter the greatest tribute. 'He (Hardy) was devoted to you. Somehow I think he might have lived had you been here... You seemed nearer to him, somehow, than anyone else, certainly more akin'.

In his final letter to Mrs Hardy in December 1932, Lawrence apologises for the fact that his translation which he had sent her of the 'Odyssey' has gone astray and promises to send another to Max Gate. The money (presumably from the sales of his book) he says is useful in that he is using it to have the 'wood-beetles eating the roof of Clouds Hill... doctored and sprayed' and the kitchen downstairs turned into 'a book-room with shelves'. Finally, if the money lasts, he hopes to have a 'bath and hot-water boiler' installed. He is sorry that 'they' - his mother and brother Bob - went to China to continue their missionary work as 'they were happy in the cottage (Clouds Hill, which they had recently visited). Perhaps they will come back'. Sadly however, Lawrence was never to see either of them again.

It was thanks to Florence Hardy that Lawrence was permitted entry to Max Gate, where he was able not only to indulge in his favourite pursuit of literary conversation and criticism but also to have a taste of home life which as a single man, he had not experienced since childhood. He described his visits there as 'a great pleasure... the greatest I have, which is why I try to keep my indulgence in it within bounds'. Perhaps this reflects a certain guilt on the latter's part about being, in his own words, 'too happy'.

Mrs Florence Hardy considered Lawrence to be 'the most marvellous man I have ever met. It is not his exploits in Arabia that attracts me, nor the fact that he is a celebrity: it is his character that is so splendid'. Hardy had hung a portrait of Lawrence on the wall of his study and Florence was sad that her husband had died whilst Lawrence was in India so the two would never meet again. On his return to England she made Lawrence a gift of a coffin-stool and the great man's fountain pen.

Chapter **32**

ROBERT GRAVES

Lawrence and Robert Ranke Graves, poet, novelist and author, met at All Souls College, Oxford in 1919 and the two became friends. Graves, born in 1895, would go on to write an autobiography 'Goodbye to All That' (1929 - about the Great War in which he served in the Army), 'I Claudius' (1934 - an historical novel about Imperial Rome), and a biography of his friend entitled 'Lawrence and the Arabs' which was published by Jonathan Cape in 1938. From 1929 onwards Graves lived mainly in Majorca.

When Graves learns that Lawrence has joined the R.A.F. and is serving in the ranks, he 'felt that he ought to be rescued' and invites the latter to go with him and his family and live out in Nepal. However although the offer sounded attractive, Lawrence declined saying 'I came here to eat dirt, till its taste is normal to me'. The R.A.F. he said, had 'the one great merit of showing me humanity very clear and clean'.

In March 1923 Lawrence informs Graves that the R.A.F has thrown him out because of 'too great publicity' and that he is now a recruit in the Tank Corps. Following a request by Lawrence, Graves is then instrumental in effecting for him an introduction to Thomas Hardy.

In 1925 we find Lawrence giving Graves a critique of 'Poetic Unreason' in which Graves uses psychology as a tool with which to interpret poetry, and in 1928 Lawrence writes to Graves from India thanking him for the two 'excellent letters you have given me about (Lawrence's own book) 'The Mint". 'In the main' said Graves 'I liked it very much, better than 'Seven Pillars' because it had been written straight off, not brooded over'. In reference to the last page of Graves's letter 'about fucking', Lawrence sheds a little more light on his own sexuality. 'I haven't ever: and don't much want to... Judging from the way people talk it's transient, if two and three-quarters or three and three-quarters or three hours and three-quarters. So I don't feel I miss much: and it must leave a dirty feeling, too'.

In 1929 Lawrence writes to Graves in glowing terms about 'Goodbye to All That'. 'This is very good. The war is the best part and completely carried on and up the excitement of the opening chapters. Most excellent. Your pictures of wounds and nerves are exactly as they should be: sane, decent, right'. 'S.S. (Siegfried Sassoon) comes out of it very well. I'm glad of that, for I like him: homosex and all'. This latter comment brings to mind the phrase 'warts and all' and suggests that Lawrence likes Sassoon in spite of him being homosexual, rather than because of it. It also implies that although Lawrence does not consider himself to be a homosexual, he can still be open and frank with Graves, whom he knows to BE a homosexual.

In April 1931 Lawrence, now based at Plymouth, writes to tell Graves, now living in Majorca with American writer and divorcee Laura Riding, about his work on 'new types of marine crafts for the R.A.F.' - the latter pair were writing a book in which was featured an autogyro, for which Lawrence was able to provide the technical information. However 'No Decency Left', published in 1932, failed to attract the attention of Hollywood as Graves and Riding had hoped, and was a commercial failure.

In February 1935 Lawrence, now in Bridlington, Yorkshire, tells Graves how he has set aside some income for retirement and spent the rest 'on friends and books and pictures and motor-bikes and joys of sorts'. Now however, when he is less than a month from retirement from the R.A.F., interest rates have fallen and left him having to make up 'about (£)700 more'. Lawrence, who helped Graves out financially on a previous occasion, notes that the former is now financially secure having published 'I Claudius' and 'Claudius the God' in the previous year, but declines his offer of assistance except as 'a reserve, only if ever I get meshed and unable to help myself'.

Lawrence goes on to tell Graves how he has recently met the producer Alexander Korda who he has dissuaded from making a film about him. Lawrence loathes 'the notion of being celluloided' -his rare visits to the cinema always deepen in him 'a sense of their superficial falsity...'

However Lawrence agrees that Graves may write his obituary for a London newspaper, which has requested it in advance for its files - or 'morgue' as Lawrence calls it - but says to Graves 'don't give too much importance to what I did in Arabia during the war. I feel that the Middle Eastern settlement put through by Winston Churchill and Young (Major Hubert Young who had been at Carchemish) and me in 1921 should weigh more than fighting'.

He talks about his present work of designing and testing rescue boats, and proudly tells Graves that 'not one type of R.A.F. boat in production is naval'. 'We have found, chosen, selected or derived our own sorts: they have three times the speed of their predecessors, less weight, less cost, more room, more safety, more seaworthiness'. Lawrence does not claim sole credit for this. 'They have grown out of the joint experience, skill and imagination of many men' he says.

Finally, referring to 'Seven Pillars', he reverts to his familiar role of self-deprecation. 'Well, I failed in that', he says, referring to the time he and Graves were together at Oxford and he 'was then trying to write; or be perhaps an artist or to be at least cerebral'. 'By measuring myself against such people as you and Augustus John, I could feel that I was not made out of the same stuff. Artists excite me and attract me; seduce me. Almost I could be an artist, but there is a core that puts on the brake'. He cannot pinpoint the reason why - 'If I knew what it was I would tell you, or become one of you. Only I can't. So I changed direction, right, and went into the R.A.F. ...'

It appears that Lawrence, 'after straightening out that Eastern tangle with Winston', is now happy with the final Arab settlement. 'How well the Middle East has done: it, more than any part of the world, had gained from that war'.

He went into the R.A.F., he tells Graves, 'to serve a mechanical purpose - not as a leader but as a cog of the machine... I have been a mechanic since, and a good mechanic, for my self-training to become an artist has widened my field of view: one of the benefits of being part of the machine is that one learns that it doesn't matter!' - which brings to mind the inscription he placed above the door of his cottage at Cloud's Hill where, written in Greek, are the words 'OU OPOVTIS' or 'Does not care'.

≪✤≫

Like Shaw we find Graves showing concern for Lawrence's welfare and the two men collaborating over their various literary creations. Lawrence's references to feeling unclean and wishing to 'eat dirt' are undoubtedly symptomatic of 'Rape Trauma Syndrome' and a legacy of the Deraa episode.

However the trauma has not entirely extinguished his ambitions - he still has a desire for literary recognition, a love of the company of artists and writers, and an enthusiasm for perfecting his rescue boats.

Thomas and Florence Hardy at Max Gate.
Photograph by Emil Otto Hope c. 1920
Courtesy of National Portrait Gallery, London

Robert Graves, by Eric Kennington c. 1918
Courtesy of National Portrait Gallery, London

Chapter 33

LADY ASTOR

Lawrence arrived back in England from India in January 1929 with 'one suit of plain clothes, and two sets of uniform, and a motor- bike'. 'I see hardly anyone' he writes 'and don't know what to say to them, when I do see them'. There followed in March one of his happiest postings, to the R.A.F. Flying Boat station at Cattewater on Plymouth Sound. The commanding officer was Wing-Commander Sydney Smith, the person who had previously been detailed to spirit Lawrence off the liner S.S.Rajputana to escape from the attentions of the press. Lawrence soon became friends with the Wing-Commander, his wife Clare and their daughter Maureen and their retinue of dogs, and they nicknamed him 'Tes'.

Lawrence was later to describe the two years he was to spend here as his 'Golden Reign'. 'It is a lovely place' he says, with a good camp 'comfortably laid out' where 'we are a happy family'. He also describes the magnificence of his new bike, given to him anonymously by the Shaws, and how it has 'taken me twice to London' in a 'fastest time 4 hours 44 minutes'.

In April 1929 Lady Nancy Astor visited Cattewater (later renamed 'Mount Batten') and the two commenced a friendship and subsequently corresponded by copious letters and telephone calls, and she enjoyed the occasional pillion ride on Lawrence's motorbike. She called him 'Aircraftman' and he called her, 'The Peeress'.

The Astor family originated in Heidelberg, Germany and John Jacob Astor, who emigrated to America, made a fortune in the fur trade and in property speculation in New York. His great-grandson, William Waldorf Astor moved to England and was created Viscount. Nancy Astor nee Langhorne, born in Virginia U.S.A in 1879, was the wife of the 2nd Viscount, also Waldorf, and the family seat was at Cliveden in Buckinghamshire. When on his father's death in 1919 her husband went to the House of Lords, Lady Astor succeeded him as Member of Parliament for Sutton, Plymouth, which constituency she held until 1945. She was the first woman M.P. to take her seat in the House of Commons.

Lawrence, one of society's poorest members - though this was partly through his own volition - admired the generosity of the philanthropic Lady Astor and her husband, saying 'You and Waldorf are two of the rich who would very easily pass through the eye of the needle, I reckon. If only the rest of us were as unselfish with our money'.

❧❧

Lawrence's letters to Lady Astor reveal his keen sense of humour and a refreshing facility not to be overawed by those of wealth and privilege.

Referring to a 'G.B.S. reading' which he hopes to attend, he says 'I will attend (probably in uniform, but I shan't mind you being differently dressed!) on the 23rd. If I do not turn up, then please blame the R.A.F. rather than my expectant self'. And describing a ride back from Cliveden when he raced a sports Bentley across the Plain 'I wished I had had a peeress or two on my flapper bracket!'

He makes reference to his poverty. 'The best way to be content in the R.A.F. is to stick close to it, taking only such reliefs as one's own pocket affords'. And again 'I cannot answer your wires, because often I have not a shilling to spare'. 'I cling to camp' he says 'because there I feel I belong. Belonging is a good feeling'.

He speaks of his mother, saying 'She writes often and at length (from China), and cries out for letters as when at home she cries out for our love... as if it could be turned on in a tap'. And he advises Lady Astor 'Don't play the mother too long to your kids, please! If you are interesting enough they will keep in touch. If not - why don't wish it!'

In March 1931 Lady Astor writes to Aircraftman Shaw 'I am arriving at Plymouth tomorrow at about three or four o'clock. This is to warn you that I shall call you up, and hope that if the weather is fine you will take me out in your boat. If it isn't fine, I should prefer pillion riding'. The boat she refers to is the 'Biscuit', a speedboat produced by the American Purdy Company, which a wealthy friend gave Lawrence the use of. He and his commanding officer Sydney Smith, whose work involves developing fast rescue launches and who manages the seaplane races for the Schneider Cup, take a keen interest in getting the boat into good working order. On her first outing, Smith is duly impressed. 'Never have I seen such antics from a speedboat. Tes (Lawrence) turned her round in her own length and showed her off like a small boy with an exciting toy'.

On the 4th of February 1931 there is a fatal accident in Plymouth Sound when a flying-boat nose-dives into the sea and it is Lawrence who dives, with the other rescuers, to recover the body of her pilot and is involved in the rescue of six others.

The 'Biscuit' demonstrates the R.A.F.'s need for a new generation of fast and manoeuvrable air-sea rescue boats which Lawrence lobbies for, and he soon finds himself involved in their development, production and testing.

In 1932 Lawrence's mother Sarah and eldest brother Bob, a medical missionary of the China Inland Mission, return to England on holiday and stay at Clouds Hill. Lady Astor makes them a present of some rugs and Lawrence makes no secret of his regret when they return to China later in the year. 'I wish these poor things hadn't this cast-iron sense of duty. They are not fit for life in rough places, and they were so quaint and happy in my Dorset cottage, improbable home as it is.' In the event, this was to be the last time that Lawrence would see them.

Lawrence's friends are anxious about what he will do when he leaves the R.A.F., which event occurs on the 26th February 1935. He is certainly subdued when he writes to Lady Astor on the 5th May from Clouds Hill 'It is quiet here now, and I feel as though I were fixed in my cottage for good. It is as I thought... something is finished with my leaving the R.A.F. It gets worse instead of healing over'.

He is offered the Secretaryship of the Bank of England, which he declines. Then Lady Astor invites him to her home at Cliveden to meet Stanley Baldwin who the following month will succeed Ramsay MacDonald as Prime Minister. 'I believe that when the Government reorganises', she tells Lawrence on the 7th of May 'you will be asked to reorganise the Defence Forces'. However her invitation is in vain. 'No: wild mares would not at present take me away from Clouds Hill' Lawrence replies. 'It is an earthly paradise and I am staying here till I feel qualified for it. Also there is something broken in the works, as I told you: my will, I think. In this mood I would not take on any job at all. So do not commit yourself to advocating me, lest I prove a non-starter. Am well, well-fed, full of company, laborious and innocent-customed. News from China (i.e. about his mother and brother) - NIL. The area is now a centre of disturbance. TES'.

෴

Whenever the opportunity arises, as it does all too infrequently, Lawrence can scarcely contain his joy at seeing Lady Astor, nine years his senior, and taking her out on his motorbike or in his boat, and the happy times spent in her company was probably as near as he was ever to come to having a fulfilling relationship with a member of the opposite sex.

Chapter 34

THE ACCIDENT

In November 1934 Lawrence is posted to the R.A.F. marine-craft station at Bridlington on the Yorkshire coast, where he continues his work on rescue boats, and in the following month he writes to John Buchan 'If you meet Mr Baldwin (the former Prime Minister) in the near future, will you please tell him that the return to the Air Force secured me by him (on your initiation) has given me the only really contented years of my life?'. Lawrence speaks of 'doing his best to raise the pride and respect of the ranks, and to make them pleased with their duties...' 'I owe the two of you more than my twelve years work (and another twelve on top of it, were I young enough) in the sheer satisfaction it has been'. And then, to Basil Liddell Hart (Lawrence's biographer), in anticipation of his forthcoming retirement, 'For myself I am going to taste the flavour of true leisure. For 46 years I have worked and been worked. Remaineth 23 years (of expectancy). May they be like Flecker's 'a great Sunday that goes on and on'' (This is a quotation from the poet James Elroy Flecker and it should read a '... calm Sunday that goes on and on).

In January 1935, a month before his retirement from the R.A.F., we find Lawrence at Bridlington, having left his 'Brough Superior' motorcycle behind at home in the garage intending to take it back to the factory as he feels he will be unable to afford to run it on his income of 25 shillings per week. Lawrence has always been passionate about motorcycles and his latest acquisition is a 1932 SS100 model registration GW2275 which he calls affectionately 'George VII' because it was the seventh he had owned. Described as a 'low-slung' machine, it is specially designed and adapted to his needs and has a smaller 19-inch rear wheel instead of a 21-inch to suit his relatively small frame. In a letter sent to the Brough factory in Nottingham after taking delivery he writes 'it is the silkiest thing I have ever ridden.'

On the 26th of February at the age of 46, he bicycles all the way from Bridlington to his cottage at Clouds Hill where he proposes to retire and pursue a career in writing. On the way south he breaks his journey at Fordingbridge, Hampshire, to call on the painter Augustus John who has completed a portrait of him in oils and also made two pencil sketches of him in charcoal. However when he returns and finds that the press are besieging his cottage, Lawrence postpones taking up residence there until the middle of March.

On May 3rd he writes to George Brough to inform him 'My last two long rides have been at 49 and 51 m.p.h. respectively. It looks as though I might yet break my neck on a B.S. (Brough Superior)'.

On May 13th Lawrence motorcycles from Clouds Hill down the road to Bovington Post Office to send off a parcel of books and a telegram. The intended recipient is the author Henry Williamson, admirer of Adolf Hitler and disciple of Sir Oswald Mosley, of whose book 'Tarka the Otter' Lawrence had written a long and detailed criticism which Williamson had much appreciated. The latter, who could see that 'the world was dropping down into war', hoped to enlist Lawrence's support for a meeting with Adolf Hitler.

The telegram, which reads 'Come tomorrow lunch cottage Bovington Camp wet fine', shows Lawrence to be in a positive frame of mind and rules out any notion, as has been suggested, that he may have been depressed or contemplating suicide at this time. He then refills with petrol at the Red Garage across the road but on his return journey he collides with one of two boy cyclists, goes over the handlebars and sustains a fractured skull from which he dies six days later without regaining consciousness. The cyclists were Albert Hargraves or 'Bert', who was a butcher's errand boy and whose father, also Albert, was a soldier at Bovington Camp, and Frank Fletcher his friend who had gone along to keep him company.

Charles Philip Allen, a Captain in the Royal Army Medical Corps, receives 'Mr T.E. Shaw and Hargraves' to the hospital at Bovington at the stated time of 'about 11.45', which is 25 minutes after the time that the accident was witnessed. It is the Captain who performs the post mortem examination on Lawrence. He describes 'a large fissured fracture 9 inches long extending from the left side of the head backwards to the middle line across the back of the skull and forward to the right side. Also small fracture of left orbital plate. The brain was severely lacerated especially on the left side.' Cause of death given is 'fracture of the skull and laceration of the brain, heart failure and congestion of the lungs.' He ventures the opinion that 'had Mr Shaw lived he would have been unable to speak and would (have) lost his memory and would have been paralysed.'

The Brough Superior is found to have suffered damage in that the right footrest is bent off and the rear brake pedal bent right back. It is said to have been found in second gear at the time, but whether this might have been altered by the impact is not known.

Lawrence's brother Arnold, a reader in archaeology at Cambridge who was currently in Spain, flies back from there to the hospital to be briefed by the doctors.

Bert Hargraves is detained in hospital for 11 days and his back and arms are permanently scarred by the accident. Interviewed in 1966, his mother Mrs Agnes Hargraves says that the only compensation her son had ever received for his injuries was money to replace his damaged trousers and bicycle. However she adds 'I think Lawrence was a good man. I bear his memory no grudge because of what happened to my son.'

❧

STATEMENTS FROM WITNESSES

The only independent witness, Corporal Ernest Catchpole, states at the inquest that 'At about 11.20 a.m. on May 13th 1935 I was at Clouds Hill Camping Ground (a military summer-camp with tents) and about 100 yards from the road. I heard the sound of a motorcycle coming from the direction of Bovington Camp. I saw the motorcycle which was going between 50 and 60 miles an hour. Just before the motorcycle got level with the camp it passed a black car - it was a private car and the motorcycle passed that safely. I then saw the motor cycle swerve across the road to avoid two pedal cycles going in the same direction. The motor cyclist swerved immediately after he passed the car which was going in the opposite direction.' Catchpole then describes hearing a crash and seeing the motor cycle 'twisting and turning over and over along the road'. 'I immediately went to the road and called for help. I found the motorcyclist lying on the right side of the road. His face was covered in blood and I sent to the camp for a stretcher. An army lorry came along and I asked them to take the injured persons to hospital which they did. One of the pedal cyclists was lying some distance down the road on the left hand side. I did not actually see the accident happen.' On cross-examination he says the car was 'not going very fast' and that he 'did not see the pedal cyclists before the crash.' Also that the car was on its proper side of the road.

Albert Hargraves aged 14, the butcher's errand boy, states that he was 'riding 4 to 5 feet behind Fletcher (his companion) on the left hand side of the road. I heard the sound of a motorcycle coming from behind. No motor car passed me about this time nor any traffic of any sort. I do not remember any more until I found myself in hospital.' They had been going at 'a normal pace with both hands on the handlebars' and 'had been riding in single file for about 80 yards.'

Frank Fletcher confirms that he was riding in front and Hargraves at the back. 'I was riding on the left of the road. When opposite Clouds Hill Camp I heard a motorcycle coming from behind. I then heard a crash and Bert's bicycle fell on top of me and knocked me off my bicycle. I got up and saw Mr Lawrence go over the handlebars of the motorcycle and fall about 5 yards in front.' He went back to Bert who gave him the butcher's account book and he saw three pennies lying on the road. Then Bert 'seemed to fall asleep.' Fletcher's story tallies with that of Hargraves and confirms that they encountered no car from the time they left Bovington Camp, they did not leave the road at all, and they that had been riding 'one behind the other for about 100 yards.'

❧❧

A POSSIBLE EXPLANATION

This evidence contains sufficient clues to tell us, even after all these years, what may have actually happened. Neither boy saw the black car which Corporal Catchpole said was going in the opposite direction and not very fast. Is it therefore possible that this car came out from the Camping Ground entrance AFTER the boys had passed it but BEFORE Lawrence reached it? If so this would explain the discrepancy in stories and also explain the car's slow speed on a straight section of road.

The reason Corporal Catchpole failed to see the boy pedal cyclists may have been because of the trees, or because they were in an dip in the road. There is in fact such a dip, the lowest point of which coincides very closely with the stone erected by the T.E. Lawrence Society at the place where Lawrence is believed to have come to grief. This dip, which may have been levelled out to some extent with improvements to the road over the years, is even today sufficiently deep to conceal cyclists (or cars for that matter) from any northbound motorcyclist coming up behind until the last minute, particularly one on a low-slung machine such as Lawrence's. Otherwise it is a straight road and the blind right hand bend which was several hundred yards further on from this spot would not have come into play.

There has been speculation as to why the owner of the black car failed to come forward after the accident. This may have been because he or she was unaware that it had occurred, and even if they had seen the accident in the rear-view mirror or heard about it subsequently through the media, they may nor have wished to be implicated in any way in the death of one of the century's most legendary and charismatic figures.

So we have the scenario of Lawrence travelling northwards along a straight road at the not excessive speed of 50 or 60 miles an hour when a black car pulls out into the road from his right. He passes it safely keeping to his left side of the road in the prescribed manner but, having been slightly distracted by the car, fails to see the two boys in the dip in the road, which we know was narrower in those days than it is today. He swerves, but is too late, and hits the rearmost bicycle, that of Hargraves, which is severely damaged. His brakes may have locked but this is unlikely as manufacturer George Brough examined the motorcycle afterwards and found no structural or mechanical failure. A crash helmet might have saved him but it was not his custom ever to wear one.

FURTHER EVIDENCE IN FAVOUR OF THE 'ACCIDENT' THEORY'

In 1985 a reporter from the 'Bournemouth Evening Echo' went to interview Frank Fletcher who now resided at Wandsworth, London. 'The road wasn't like it is now at that time' said Fletcher. 'They've widened it since then, added a lot to each side. And there were hills on it. When you come out of Bovington Camp the hill is the same. Then you've got your straight bit of road first of all and then it dipped down a bend a wee bit more and then up again. Well the second dip, that's gone. That second dip, we were just above that - a few yards along, he couldn't have seen us like.' Fletcher remained adamant that there was no black car and his story then was very similar to the one he had given at the inquest fifty years previously in May 1935. 'My mate heard the motorcycle coming up behind us. We were riding side by side at the time and then I moved in. And then we only went along another 20 yards or so when, wooff, it hit the back of my mate's bike and then hit mine, though there was no damage to mine and I went over to one side. The motorbike itself skidded along the road - I thought it was going to explode. And then all of a sudden when I straightened myself up and looked round I saw my mate unconscious. I saw Mr Lawrence go over the handlebars and the bike skid along the road. It wasn't very wide a road, more like a track then, and he was sitting up against a tree facing Bovington Camp. So I went across to him and saw blood on his face. The next thing I knew that the soldiers came and an ambulance, which must have come from the camp. After I told my parents my dad came back later from the camp and told me who he was (i.e. T.E. Lawrence). I didn't know at the time, nobody did. And then the newspaper men came. I was offered a shilling and sixpence for the story - it was quite a bit of money in those days. I went down to the hospital to see Bertie (Hargraves) but I was too young and they wouldn't let me in. We went down to the inquest and Corporal Catchpole brought it up about the black car and that and they asked me questions, and (I) said there definitely wasn't a black car at all. Bert was definitely behind me, because he was the one that told me to get to the side of the road in front of him.'

Nancy – Viscountess Astor, by John Singer
Sargent, 1923
Courtesy of National Portrait Gallery, London

Lawrence on 'Boanerges' (The sons of thunder)
Courtesy of Bodleian Library, University of Oxford

Chapter 35

THE FUNERAL

After the inquest in the morning of May 21st 1935, Lawrence's funeral was held in the afternoon at the Church of St. Nicholas, Moreton. Mourners of whom there were many included Florence Hardy, Mr and Mrs Winston Churchill, Augustus John, Lady Astor, Mr and Mrs Siegfried Sassoon, Aircraftman Bradbury of the R.A.F. and Private Russell of the Royal Tank Corps. Also present were representatives of the King of Iraq and the Emir Abdulla of Transylvania. The Shaws were absent on a cruise to South Africa, as was E.M. Forster who later visited Clouds Hill with the Sassoons. Neither Trenchard nor Allenby nor Robert Graves attended. Feisal had died in Switzerland two years before, and there was no representative of Lawrence's late father's family the Chapmans. His brother Arnold was present but not his mother Sarah and brother Bob, who were on their way home from China and did not yet know of his death.

The same day a message from King George Vth to Arnold Lawrence was published in The Times newspaper. It read 'The King has heard with sincere regret of the death of your brother, and deeply sympathises with you and your family at this sad loss. Your brother's name will live in history, and the King gratefully recognises his distinguished services to his country and feels that it is tragic that the end should have come in this manner to a life still so full of promise.'

The inscription on the tombstone, erected by his mother on her return to England, reads as follows -

TO THE DEAR MEMORY OF
T.E.LAWRENCE
FELLOW OF ALL SOVLS COLLEGE
OXFORD
BORN 16 AVGVST 1888
DIED 19 MAY 1935
THE HOVR IS COMING & NOW IS
WHEN THE DEAD SHALL HEAR
THE VOICE OF THE
SON OF GOD
AND THEY THAT HEAR
SHALL LIVE

In May 1985 a mysterious note appeared on the grave which read 'I have kept the secret still.'

Delivered annually to the Moreton Church rectory on the anniversary of Lawrence's birthday, August 16th, is a bunch of white roses with one less bloom for each year - in 1984 for example there were 36 roses. In 1993 the message which accompanied the roses, which in that year numbered 27, read 'In memory of T.E.S. 2020 AD' (the 'S' stands presumably for Shaw, his adopted surname), which points to the date of 2019 as the one on which the final rose will be delivered and to the intriguing date of 2020 when deliveries will presumably cease. Another flower delivered annually and anonymously is a geranium.

In August 1990 there appeared an article by Gerard Kemp in the 'Sunday Express' newspaper which described an interview he had conducted with a Doctor Susan Lawrence, a 35 year old cancer specialist from California, who confessed to having changed her name to 'Lawrence' and 'to being related in a way. I can't say any more or my confidentiality will be violated.' She also confessed to having seen David Lean's film 'Lawrence of Arabia' 'at least 12 times.' 'I fly over (to England) three times a year, each time for a week, for the anniversaries of Lawrence's death on May 19 and his birth on August 16' she said. Her third visit always coincided with a date in November which was the anniversary of the rape of Lawrence by Turkish soldiers in Deraa. She had visited the latter place and described Lawrence as having 'showed all the classic signs of being a rape victim.' However Doctor Lawrence denied that it was she who sends the box of white roses which appear on the grave every year.

The company Interflora which delivers the flowers has confirmed that the order for the flowers comes from America and is due to end in the year 2020.

The late Rector of Wareham, the Reverend Lionel Howe, referred in a letter donated to St. Martin's Church by his widow, to 'old Mrs

Lawrence (i.e Sarah), whom we later (after the funeral) met and stood in awe of, I think E.K. (Eric Kennington the sculptor and friend of Lawrence who was responsible for the lettering on his tombstone and the effigy of him in Wareham church) considers her rather 'a holy terror'. The Reverend Howe said that 'if anyone put flowers on 'Ned's' grave at Moreton and she found them, she would fling them over the hedge. But I remember her once coming to the rectory at Wareham and admiring a plant in bloom and in full flower and I said would she like some and she said she would, and we learned later that she had put them on T.E.'s grave herself. E.K. told us that in her eyes Ned was almost God-like and she had wanted his memorial to take the form of a huge pyramid somewhere in the Desert!'

And so with the identity of the rose-donor still unknown and the date of '2020' enigmatic and yet supposedly significant, the mystery which attached to so much of Lawrence's life was to continue after his death.

Chapter **36**

FATE OF HIS FAMILY

Sarah Lawrence outlived her husband by forty years and died in 1959 at the age of ninety eight. Was her legacy to the young 'Ned' to leave him as a battered child? Did her son show the typical features of a child who has suffered prolonged violence and emotional deprivation, as described so well by Jan Carter in 'The Maltreated Child'. Did he become institutionalised in his home, retarded in speech, inhibited in play and frozen in his relationships with other people? The answer to all these questions is clearly 'No'.

As with so many aspects of Ned's life there are no clear cut answers, but the publication of letters written by him in later years to his friend Charlotte, the wife of George Bernard Shaw, shed more light on his enigmatic personality.

The use of the words 'very exciting' by Ned in respect of his mother, a person who he believed was attempting to smother and destroy him by trying to enter into his very psyche, at first seems paradoxical unless explained in psycho-sexual terms.

As George Bernard Shaw pointed out, corrective punishment by beating can be an outlet for both the sadistic impulses of the beater and also the masochistic impulses of the beaten, or be in his own words, a 'final triumph of the vice it pretends to repress'. It therefore seems likely that Ned, who like his brothers was deliberately deprived of female company by his mother and therefore had no opportunity to develop normal male-female relationships, was referring to her beatings when he used the words 'very exciting' and it was this which stimulated in him a latent erotic tendency.

Much has been made of Ned's illegitimacy and some have even argued that his attempts to minimise its importance are an indication of just how adversely the knowledge of it affected him. There is no doubt that in those days it carried a considerable social stigma and the person born out-of-wedlock might find him or herself precluded from attending certain schools or being appointed to certain professional or governmental posts as well as having to endure social isolation and ostracism.

However this image of the guilt-ridden, self-hating introvert angry with his parents for never having told him directly the truth about his illegitimacy and for espousing Christian values when they themselves were actually 'living in sin', does not easily equate with his subsequent achievements - at school, in travel, study for degree, archaeological digs, holidays of exploration and the Arabian campaign in the desert. Neither is it borne out by the positive tone of the letters he sent home from abroad. Instead we have the impression of an enthusiastic young man with an enquiring mind who is happy and fulfilled in what he is doing. Why, therefore, should we not take his own statement, that he knew the truth about his illegitimacy before he was ten and 'didn't care a straw', at face value?

It was on April the 7th 1919 when Lawrence was at the Paris Peace Conference that he received news that his father Thomas had been taken ill with pneumonia. He straightaway returned home only to find that his father had already died.

Ned was clearly fond of his father, despite the fact that, as the former put it, his mother had 'remodelled' the latter and Thomas had gone along with it to keep in with her. Their shared bicycling holidays is proof of this, and Ned's interest in mediaeval chivalry - which may well have had its roots in the fact that his paternal ancestors had once owned great and ancient estates in Ireland - was fostered by his father particularly in regard to churches and castles. Ned's researches would have transported him into the realms of knights and their notion of asceticism - the renunciation of physical pleasure for the deliberate seeking out of discomfort and pain - often for religious reasons.

As already stated, the eldest brother Bob became a medical missionary with the China Inland Mission. He died in 1971. The third brother Will and the fourth brother Frank both lost their lives in the Great War. The fifth brother Arnold, who was the only one of the five to marry, became a classical archaeologist and professor. He lived for some years in Ghana where he established a museum, and died on Easter Sunday 1991 aged 90 years.

Chapter 37

FATE OF HIS FRIENDS

Lord Kitchener died in June 1916 when HMS Hampshire, which was carrying him on an urgent visit to Russia, was mined and sank off the Orkney Islands. Lawrence would have been gratified that he and Kitchener shared the same views as to the importance of Sinai and immensely grateful for the support of the latter for Emir Abdullah's notion of an Arab uprising.

To what extent Kitchener was privy to the Sykes-Picot agreement, prior to its being made public by the Russians in November 1917 following their recent Bolshevic Revolution, and also of the Balfour declaration affirming that the British Government was in favour of the establishment of a Jewish national homeland in Palestine, is not known. At any event his premature death was to preclude him from having any influence over post-war events in the Middle East.

❧❧

Lawrence's relationship with Emir Feisal was dogged by the knowledge that the British planned all along ultimately to betray him. Prior to Feisal's meeting with Allenby following the fall of

Damascus, Lawrence admits that he had 'already betrayed the (Sykes-Picot) treaty's existence to Feisal', and as early as June 1917 had written on army message forms 'We are calling them (the Arabs) to fight for us on a lie and I can't stand it'.

Shortly after arriving back in England Lawrence was urging the Eastern Committee of the War Cabinet of which he was a member to give Syria autonomy under Feisal's rule, and as far as the Jews were concerned took the view that the Arabs would accept their 'infiltration' into Palestine provided it 'remained in British hands' and did not become an independent Jewish state.

When in November 1918 Feisal went to France to tour that country and be introduced to the French president, Lawrence was dispatched to Marseilles to warn him that the French were plotting to keep him away from the Peace Conference. When Feisal arrived in England on December 9th, Lawrence arranged for him to meet the Zionist leader Chaim Weizmann to discuss the latter's aspirations in Palestine. It was during his three weeks in England that Feisal, in the company of Lawrence, met King George V.

Lawrence's enthusiasm for Feisal as the man with the character and charisma to unite the disparate Arab tribesmen in their struggle against the Turks was only matched by his profound disappointment at the perceived betrayal of him and his fellow Arabs by Britain after the war.

Sherif Hussein's failure to accept Lawrence's persuasive attempts to make him agree to the terms of the Cairo Peace Settlement following the Allied victory in 1918 opened the door to Ibn Saud of Riyadh, who had always resisted the Sherif's claim to be King of the Hejaz and whose Wahabi tribesmen had defeated the Sherif's forces in May 1919. In 1924 Ibn Saud ousted the Sherif, forcing him to flee into exile in Cyprus. However Lawrence was successful in propping up the shaky regime of the Sherif's son Abdullah in Trans-Jordania (now Jordan).

Lawrence's great patience in the face of the Sherif's unpredictable behaviour and his constant squabbling with his son Emir Feisal was to no avail. Had an accommodation been reached, then the Sherif's self-proclaimed kingship of the Hejaz might well have become a permanent reality.

❦

It was Gertrude Bell to whom Lawrence gave credit for persuading him to publish his book 'Seven Pillars'. Having agonised over whether or not it was good enough, it was Bell's words 'Wouldn't you consider publishing it for your friends?' that finally turned the tide.

After the Arab rebellion in Mesopotamia and its suppression with much bloodshed in the summer of 1920, Bell was critical of what she regarded as the misleading statements Lawrence was making in the press. Although aware of Lawrence's support for the family of Sherif

Hussein, self-proclaimed King of the Hejaz, she was especially worried by his failure to recognise the strength of his rival Ibn Saud and cautioned him saying 'You can't guard the Hejaz by backing Hussein and dropping I.S.'

Miss Bell, who attended the Paris Peace Conference with Lawrence, described him as 'the most picturesque' figure there. The two of them worked together to put the case for the installation of Feisal as King of Iraq and, as Lawrence wrote to Mrs Charlotte Shaw in 1927, Gertrude Bell 'swung all the Mespot. British officials to the Feisal solution, whilst Winston (Churchill) and I swung the English people'.

After the Conference, Miss Bell served with the military administration and later with the Government of Iraq under the British Mandate as Assistant Political Officer, and Lawrence wrote of her noble support for Feisal and of how 'Her Baghdad letter gives a splendid idea of him in action as a ruler'.

Gertrude Bell died in Baghdad on 12th July 1926, where she had held the post of Director of Antiquities.

Although Gertrude Bell saw Lawrence as impetuous and believed, rightly as it transpired, that he had misread the situation in the Hejaz and had underestimated the strength of Sherif Hussein's rival Ibn Saud, nevertheless she was broadly in agreement with his aims for Arab self-determination. Also it is doubtful whether, without her encouragement, he would have gone on to publish his masterpiece 'Seven Pillars'.

అఖ్య

Dr Hogarth died on 6th November 1927 and we rely on Lawrence's own words to describe his affection for his late mentor, inspiration and friend, who took over the role of father to him when his own father died in 1919, and the debt he owed him. In a letter he subsequently wrote to Mrs Shaw he said '... the background to my life before I enlisted has gone. Hogarth sponsored my first tramps in Syria - then put me on the staff for Carchemish, which was a golden place...' '... whenever I was in a dangerous position I used to make up my mind after coming away from his advice'. In the same year he wrote 'The death of D.G.H. seems to have flattened me out, rather. He was like a reserve, always there behind me, if I got flustered or puzzled. And now I have no confidence.'

Six weeks later Lawrence's grief was undiminished. 'My bed-fellows (In the R.A.F., which he had rejoined in August 1925) tell me that I cry in bed at nights,' he told Mrs Shaw, 'in the early hours of the night before they go to sleep and before I wake up. They begin to suspect me of secret griefs'. And in a letter to Edward Garnett '... I saw little of him (Hogarth) in the last five years; but the knowledge of that tower of understanding fellowship was reserve to me, and I felt orphaned at his going'. '... Hogarth carried his rareness in his mouth and eyes; - and he is wholly lost'.

Hogarth was 'the parent I could trust without qualification, to understand what bothered me'. He was 'humane, and knew the length and breadth of human nature, and understood always, without judging'.

And in 1928 he wrote 'Yes, Hogarth's going was a bad knock to me. I relied on him, always, to know where I was at, and why, without being told: and, for his existence there, I like Oxford'. To the artist William Rothenstein he wrote 'Oxford was to me a beautiful place, and a home, because he (Hogarth) lived there, for me to see for a few minutes whenever I passed'.

And as for Hogarth, this affection was amply reciprocated, as is evident from a letter he wrote to his wife in November 1917 when Lawrence was engaged in raids on the Hejaz railway. 'He... is away on a risky venture, and I'll be more than glad to see him out of it... I only hope and trust TEL will get back safe. He is out and up against it at this moment. If he comes through it's a V.C. (Victoria Cross) - if not - well, I don't care to think about it!'

When Lawrence returned safely to Akaba, Hogarth informed his wife that the French had awarded him the Croix de Guerre with palms. Lawrence's response to this was 'The French Government has stuck another medal on me... I wish they would not bother, but they never consult one before doing these things'.

In 1920 Hogarth, referring to the Arab Revolt, summed up by saying 'It would not have begun but for Kitchener's invitation in the first instance, and assurance of British support in the second; it could not have been sustained without the money, food-stuffs and munitions of which Great Britain provided; it might never have spread beyond the Hejaz but for the long sight and audacious action of Lawrence; and it won through to Damascus only as a flying right wing of Allenby's last drive'.

In 1923 Lawrence made Hogarth his literary executor and when his book 'Revolt in the Desert' was published in March 1927, it would make a sizeable profit and enable Lawrence, then in financial difficulty, not only to clear his debts but also to make substantial donations to the R.A.F. Memorial Fund and also help his fellow airmen and friends. The consequence of his generosity however, was to leave him malnourished and virtually destitute.

In 1924 when Hogarth's health was failing, Lawrence wrote to his friend Charlotte Shaw of this 'very kind, very wise, very loveable man... All my opportunities, all those I've wasted, came directly or indirectly, out of his trust in me'.

Hogarth's widow Laura wrote to Lawrence about her late husband 'I know that you will miss him, more than perhaps anyone else, except Billie and me'.

∞

Allenby, Winston (Churchill), and the Chief of Air Staff Sir Hugh Trenchard were described by Lawrence in 1928 as his 'gallery of chiefs', or in other words the three men he most admired and respected, 'to date'. Lawrence, who typically was in no way overawed by Churchill, showed a personal touch when he wrote in November 1922 to commiserate with him over the latter's loss of his Dundee seat in the General Election and advised him to take a holiday. Lawrence's relationship with Churchill, which might on occasion be considered as showing over-familiarity and a certain lack of deference, was typical of the man and this behaviour on his part may have been a legacy of his illegitimacy. In other words, by treating everyone else as an equal, he desired that they in turn would treat him as an equal, regardless of his past.

In August 1927 Lawrence wrote to Ralph Isham, an American who had served as a British officer in France and who he had met in 1919. 'Did I tell you that I consider what I did in Arabia morally indefensible. So I refused pay and decorations while it lasted, and will not take any personal profit out of it: neither from a book about it; nor will I take any position which depends on my war reputation. 'Arabia barred". This helps to explain not only the impecunious position which Lawrence found himself in after the war ended, but also his failure to grasp the opportunities offered to him later by Churchill.

In 1931 there is more praise for Churchill in a letter from Lawrence to Henry T. Russell the United Press Correspondent. 'As for the Arab business: I had a hateful war: and after 2½ years of a dog-fight with the British Cabinet to secure the fulfilment of the promises to which they made me an unwilling and post-facto accessory. When Winston Churchill fulfilled all that was humanly attainable of those promises I was free to quit events and return to the class and mode of life that I belong to and feel happy in'.

However even Churchill's efforts on behalf of the Arabs do not appear totally to have expunged Lawrence's sense of guilt about his part in the affair. In 'Seven Pillars' he describes looking back to August 1918 and his 30th birthday. 'It came to me queerly how, four years ago, I had meant to be a general and knighted, when thirty. Such temporal dignities (if I survived the next four weeks) were now in my grasp - only that the sense of the falsity of the Arab position had cured me of a crude ambition: while it left me craving for a good repute among men... Here were the Arabs believing in me, Allenby trusting me, my bodyguard dying for me: and I began to wonder if all established reputations were founded, like myself, on fraud'.

A major factor underlying the debate over the post-war division of the Middle East was that oil had been found in Iraq and was needed in ever increasing quantities, and it was in the national interest of both Britain and France to exercise control of it. A measure of the commercial importance attached to the region is that Sir Arnold Wilson, former deputy chief political officer in Baghdad, later became the chairman of the Mesopotamian Oil Company and it transpired that the American archaeologist William Yale turned out to be a senior member of the Standard Oil Company of California.

Chapter **38**

THE EFFIGY

In the spring of 1920 Lawrence purchased two portraits of soldiers by Eric Henri Kennington R.A. (born in 1888), sculptor and official war artist, at a London exhibition and left his All Souls address. Kennington subsequently visited Lawrence at Oxford, and was told by him that he required illustrations of some of the English and Arab participants in the Revolt for his book. Kennington subsequently visited the Middle East to make portraits at first hand of some of Lawrence's comrades-in-arms and subsequently became Art Editor of the splendid subscriber's edition of 'Seven Pillars' which was published in 1926.

Lawrence was to remain friends with Kennington and in August 1934 wrote to him in his familiar self-deprecatory way saying 'Both the 'Seven Pillars' and 'The Mint' stink of personality... One of the sorest things in life is to come to realise that one is just not good enough. Better perhaps than some, than many, almost - but I do not care for relatives, for matching myself against my kind. There is an ideal standard somewhere and only that matters: and I cannot find it. Hence this aimlessness'. And anticipating his forthcoming retirement 'Out I go. Clouds Hill awaits me, as home and I have nearly £2 a week of an income. So I mean to digest all the leisure I can enjoy: and if I find that doing nothing is not worse than this present futile being busy about what doesn't matter - why then, I shall go on doing nothing. But if doing nothing is not good - why then, I shall cast loose again and see where I bring up'.

On 6th of May 1935 he expresses to Kennington from Clouds Hill sentiments that perhaps many would share after having been retired for two months. . 'You wonder what I am doing? Well, so do I, in truth. Days seem to dawn, suns to shine, evenings to follow, and then I sleep. What I have done, what I am doing, what I am going to do, puzzle me and bewilder me. Have you ever been a leaf and fallen from your tree in autumn and been really puzzled about it? That's the feeling'. Only fifteen days later Kennington was to be one of the pall-bearers at Lawrence's funeral.

The story of the Lawrence effigy was told by its creator Eric Kennington on July 3rd 1945 at Wareham. The monument was commissioned by the Lawrence family through T. E. Lawrence's younger brother Arthur Walter Lawrence and designed originally as a national memorial for Westminster Abbey, but as there was already a bust of Lawrence also by Kennington in St. Paul's crypt, it was considered superfluous.

Kennington stated, 'The shock of T.E.'s death, yes, when we were getting over it I had a letter from Buxton (Robin Buxton, Lawrence's banker and former comrade-in-arms in Arabia) asking me to attend a committee meeting which would plan a national memorial. We met. I attended. As far as I can remember the other members were Buxton in the chair, Lady Astor who soon elbowed him out of it and was in it herself, Newcombe (Captain S.F. Newcombe of the Royal Engineers and formerly director of the Sinai survey), Storrs (Sir Ronald Storrs, formerly assistant to the British High Commissioner in Cairo), Lionel Curtis (administrator and political theorist who popularised the idea of a commonwealth of self-governing nations), Bernard Shaw, Sir Herbert Baker (architect, who provided Lawrence with the attic room in Barton Street, Westminster where he wrote much of 'Seven Pillars')... They said we should make a national appeal. Then Baker said he had asked T.E. once what his idea was for a monument to himself and his reply 'the largest mountain in Arabia carved into a likeness of himself.' I lay low till Baker said 'What about an effigy. We have a distinguished sculptor here.' That was the only meeting I attended but I was told my drawings had been accepted and I was to go ahead and await official confirmation. Next I wrote to A. W. Lawrence who can be spiteful and vindictive. He came and saw the effigy. 'What's this worth to you' he said. My answer was 'Two thousand pounds.' He pulled out a cheque book and wrote out a cheque for two thousand pounds.

'Now it's mine and I can do what I like with it.' We went to Salisbury (cathedral) and looked at the site and met the Dean. He was against it. He said he wanted it in the south transept on a high table-tomb. A.W. explained to him elaborately and architecturally that this was an effigy in the Early English style and flattish for putting on a low base not like the fifteenth century figures, all knobbly and sticking up so you could see them from below. Of course he was right, but the Dean thought the height of the building demanded a tall base with a raised up figure... Then we went and saw the Bishop at the palace. A.W. wasn't giving in, nor was the Dean (terrible fellow.) So having slain a bishop, murdered a dean, turned down a cathedral, A.W. quite ruthless said 'We'll go to Wareham.' We fairly danced and said 'This is the place - St. Martin's, Wareham' (the 10th century church of St. Martin's on the Walls.) Then back to Salisbury to tell the Bishop. He was a bit surprised to see us back so soon. He was delighted and said 'I've always loved that church and from the first I thought it was the right place for the Lawrence effigy.'

Richard Knowles (formerly of R.A.F. Cattewater, Plymouth) gives an excellent description of the effigy, which is carved from a three ton block of Portland stone. Lawrence is represented in his Arab robes and head dress from the fabled period of his involvement with the Arab Revolt during the First World War. The right hand rests on the hilt of his dagger whilst the left lies loosely at his side. His feet rest upon a piece of

Hittite sculpture representing his pre-war archaeological days at Carchemish, his head lies on a camel saddle and beside it are three unlabelled books which represent those carried with him on the Arab Campaign - 'Morte d'Arthur', the 'Oxford Book of English Verse', and the 'Greek Anthology'. The chest upon which the effigy lies carries only the simple text 'T.E. Lawrence 1888-1935'. The effigy is in an unashamed English fourteenth century style with crossed legs, the Arab robes being treated rather as the medieval gown.

Wing Commander Reginald G. Sims (with whom Lawrence had worked at Bridlington and who was an expert amateur photographer) photographed the sculpture at its various stages of development, and Kennington said of the results 'The photos are welcome. I profit by these. They show me errors.' Undoubtedly it was this help from Sims which enabled Kennington to produce the exquisite likeness of Lawrence which he did.

Roses on Lawrence's grave.
Courtesy the Rector of Moreton

The Effigy
Courtesy the Rector of Wareham

EPILOGUE

Lawrence's heroic exploits during the Great War, which were of immense value to the Allied cause, are well documented but today it is the man within who continues to fascinate and intrigue.

Lawrence appears to have had a closer relationship with his father, with whom he shared an interest in archaeology and photography, than did his brothers. For instance there is only one reference to another brother joining the two of them for a bicycle ride. We may speculate that perhaps his mother Sarah was jealous of this closeness and that is one of the reasons which led her to beat him more frequently than she did them.

When a person is continually picked on or victimised, that person can become consumed with guilt, and believe that they have deserved it and are therefore unworthy of any other treatment. This theme of 'unworthiness' runs throughout most of Lawrence's adult life and could account for the fact that whereas he hated to see other people being bullied, he was unable to stand up for himself. In his book 'The Mint' he cannot bear to see the underdog being downtrodden and diminished and has physically to restrain himself from punching the corporals and sergeant majors in the R.A.F. when they bully his fellow aircraftmen. In his writings he rails against injustice on behalf of others, and yet accepts bullying and punishment himself and his avoidance of eye-contact has the effect of goading the bully to even further excesses.

Clearly Lawrence looked upon Dahoum the donkey boy as a son, and perhaps the only way he could contemplate having a son of his own was by 'adoption', since he did not get on well with women as prospective partners. This it would seem was largely the result of his mother's treatment of him, and her dislike of girls, and the strenuous efforts she made to keep any prospective female partner away from Ned and his brothers. Therefore with four brothers and an overbearing mother, he would have had little or no female company and no insight into the way the female mind works, and so it suited him to disappear into a world of asceticism and as far as his sexuality is concerned, live a kind of monk-like existence.

This may be why Lawrence could be so dedicated to the Arab cause - it gave him a purpose that demanded his all, so he could avoid the necessity of having to address the problem of the opposite sex. This does not mean that he was homosexual. There is no evidence to support this view and it is less than charitable of people to interpret his discomfiture with prospective female partners in this way. He was a sensitive and honourable man, and like all of us he needed a purpose in life.

Dahoum came to him like a 'ready-made' son. He was a young man and of an age where his mind was like a blank sheet of paper ready to be written on. He had intelligence and a good and loyal nature, and Lawrence could see his potential and wanted to influence and help this young man in the way that a father would his son. Lawrence was aware of and sensitive to the differences in their two cultures, and did not wish to change this basis, just add to it by providing extra education and opportunity. Hence the letter from Lawrence to his mother in which he stated that he did not wish Dahoum to be coerced away from his Islamic faith.

Lawrence's fierce support for and defence of the Arabs was probably as much for Dahoum as for anyone else - it was a father fighting for his son's cause - and when Lawrence learned that Dahoum had died waiting for him, he would have felt all his energy drain out of him for a while as his hopes and dreams died with the boy. He would have been left with a feeling of guilt, that somehow he had let Dahoum down and could have prevented his death, which is a normal stage of all grief particularly if the person is not there when the loved one dies. This would have increased his feeling of worthlessness.

And yet Lawrence persevered, and continued to fight for the Arabs' freedom as a sort of memorial to Dahoum - a purpose to go on in his memory. Yet this was to mean that when, in Lawrence's eyes, the British ultimately failed the Arabs, he would feel it as a personal failure to the memory of someone he had loved like a son, and so would be left with even greater feelings of disloyalty and unworthiness.

Perhaps his subsequent decision to go into the ranks in the R.A.F. and the Army was a way of punishing himself for his self-perceived unworthiness, because he could not bear the thought that he had let Dahoum down and, despite all the effort he had invested in the cause he believed in, had failed to achieve the goal he had hoped for.

œž

Superimposed upon the unhappy and unsatisfactory legacy left to him by his mother which, it must be said, did not prevent him from fulfilling himself in every way except personally and emotionally, and the further trauma he suffered with the death of Dahoum, was an added trauma more devastating to his psyche than either of the former, namely that of the rape at Deraa. Although at Deraa Lawrence had physically resisted the Turkish Bey and in so doing provided the catalyst for his punishment-beating and subsequent rape, he managed to convince himself that he had in fact submitted to it voluntarily. And thereafter as the years went by the classical symptoms of 'Rape Trauma Syndrome' intensified in him, and Lawrence became increasingly depressed and lost his independence of mind, and with it the power to determine his own future. The Lawrence of old, whose vision and energy knew no bounds, had gone forever.

A vivid account of the feelings of a man who has been raped by another man is given by Christopher B. Smith who was assaulted at gunpoint in the back of a truck in October 1994 when he was aged 24. 'Humiliation', 'cheap', 'degraded', 'used', 'abused' or 'violated' did not begin to describe how he felt. He described his soul as being 'engulfed with turmoil and pain'. Once back at home he removed his clothes and threw them into the wash, then scrubbed himself in the shower 'harder than I ever had before' so that 'with each stroke, the scalding hot water washed another layer of filth and disgust that covered me down the drain.' The more the police officers questioned him about the rape, the more he believed that he was responsible for what happened. That he deserved it. That he wanted it. 'I felt stripped of every ounce of masculinity that I once possessed' he said. 'After all, the majority of the world just might believe that a "real man" would not allow this to happen to him.'

Even two years later, for Smith there were times when he felt his heart was going to break, and times when there was an unbearable sadness in his soul. For him the saddest reality was that the 'victimisation that occurs as a result of a crime such as rape does not end at the completion of the crime. It follows the victim home. It dwells in the examining room of hospitals. It thrives in courtrooms and police districts. It lingers in the lives of victims everywhere and shapes their lives.'

And yet for Lawrence, who must have experienced all these feelings, his spirit somehow endured and he continued to take pleasure in the secluded cottage he loved so well, and in his beloved music and the company of his literary and artistic friends.

∾∾

Even today male rape remains a taboo subject, but even so one would like to think that nowadays, instead of being despised and vilified, this once strong, purposeful and heroic man would have received the support he so desperately needed when in his latter years he became dejected, confused and rudderless.

∾∾

How will Lawrence be judged by future generations? Lawrence met Winston Churchill for the last time at Chartwell in March 1935 when he was trying to enlist his help in dissuading the newspaper men from besieging him at his Clouds Hill cottage, and perhaps Churchill himself should have the final word. 'Alike in his great period of adventure and command or in those later years of self-suppression and self-imposed eclipse' wrote Churchill about Lawrence 'he always reigned over those with whom he came in contact. They felt themselves in the presence of an extra-ordinary being. They felt that his latent reserves of force and will-power were beyond measurement. If he roused himself to action, who should say what crisis he could not surmount or quell? If things were going very badly, how glad one would be to see him come round the corner. Part of the secret of his stimulating ascendancy lay, of course, in his disdain for most of the prizes, the pleasures and comforts of life'. And Churchill ends by saying, 'King George the Fifth wrote to Lawrence's brother 'His name will live in history.' That is true. It will live in English letters, it will live in the traditions of the Royal Air Force, it will live in the annals of war and the legends of Arabia.'

And so we are left with the abiding image of sun streaming in through the stained glass window of a little church in Wareham onto the effigy of a man whose face, once so tortured and tormented, is at last serene and at peace.